The Upside of Down

JOSEPH M. STOWELL

The Upside of Down

FINDING HOPE WHEN IT HURTS

MOODY PRESS
CHICAGO

*Gratefully dedicated
to the twenty alumni
of the Moody Bible Institute who,
in the course of their service to Christ,
gave their lives as martyrs for the cause.
These honored servants,
of whom this world is not worthy,
have suffered, like Christ,
to the shedding of their own blood.
They live on in our hearts
as a penetrating reminder
that not only is Christ
worth living for,
He is worth dying for.*

Contents

With Appreciation

A special thanks goes to the many who have helped make this book possible.

First, thanks to those who have suffered much and have permitted me to be a partner with them in the process as I have stood by their side, hoping to encourage them to look for the growth and glory. I appreciate their willingness, as well, to let all of us who read this book hear their stories, that somehow we may not feel totally alone in our struggle.

Much of the credit for this book goes to my secretary, Betty McIntyre, who helped to oversee the typing and preparation of the manuscript and who was helped by Chris Criel, Connie Leeper, Tammie Merry, Andrea Miller, and Pat Zimmermann.

Thanks as well to the good people at Moody Press, who under Greg Thornton's capable leadership, take projects like this and bring them to a sensible end. Greg is assisted by Ella Lindvall, who manages the process, and Anne Scherich, who is my patient editor; as well as by Dave DeWit, whose production schedule is victimized by my tendency to push the deadlines, and his assistant, Carolyn McDaniel, a skilled typographer. To Jim Bell, Duncan Jaenicke, and Bill Thrasher for their encouragement, Thank you.

Needless to say, this project would never have been completed if my family had not been understanding through the rigors of bringing it to completion. So to Martie, my partner of twenty-five years, and to Joe, Libby, and Matt, a special thanks.

But beyond this, we all owe deep gratitude to our Lord and Savior, Jesus Christ, who came not to reign in comfort and ease but rather as Savior to suffer, that by His stripes we might be healed. If He had not led the way through the path of sorrow, we would surely be without hope.

Introduction

Getting through a season of trouble is a lot like sur-viving a roller coaster ride—except that we do not volunteer for trouble, and trouble was never intended to be fun.

Trouble is filled with stomach-wrenching drops, dips, and sudden curves. And, just when we think we've caught our breath, we're dropping again.

If we didn't know better, we might think that this roller coaster ride is a random experience, that some-how the forces that lift us up and push us down are whims of fate.

Thankfully, it is not a random ride at all. Those who understand the work of God in and through our troubles understand that He does not abandon us to di-saster. Rather, with all the strength of His character, He provides a well-engineered superstructure that sup-ports the process along a carefully planned set of tracks and guardrails. Even when the ride is too hectic, unset-tling, and twisted for us to sense the presence of His support and guidance, it still is there.

Our only hope in it all is to stay in the car and find something solid to hold onto through every turn of the experience.

The Upside of Down is about learning to trust in God's work and provision as the divine superstructure underneath every trial. It is about believing that the guiding and guarding work He performs will keep us on course.

This book is not primarily about the ultimate healing of our hurts since the end of the ride is God's responsibility. This book is, rather, about learning to respond productively in the midst of trouble. It is about finding those things that we can cling to with certainty. It is about understanding the ultimate purpose behind our suffering so that we will be willing to stay on board.

This is a book about hope—hope in that which is wonderfully solid and real. It is about hope in God, who works all things toward that which is good and who never wastes our sorrows.

1

The Upward, Inward Look
Choosing to Trust

Standing by her bed, ready to break the news that her baby had not made it through the night, I only hoped she wouldn't ask, "Why?" I had no answer to that question. I could only speak of "who"—of "Him"—and of "what" He had done.

There were just a few things Debbie could cling to that were certain, safe, and sure. Though she would feel the press of the cascading, unanswerable whys and the despair of all that was uncertain; though she would no doubt wrestle with self-punishing thoughts; though seasons of anger and self-pity would seek to lengthen their unwelcome stay; she could cling to a few certain exclamation points. If she would, she would make it through.

Though it would be different now—never again so naive, so unsuspecting, so believing that trouble was what happened to someone else—she would make it.

She and David did. Richer. Deeper. Riper. Fuller. More realistic. More able to help and heal others. More capable and ready to understand. More deeply in love with their Father in heaven. They now knew what it meant to give up a son.

It was late Saturday night, the night when pastors like to get a good sleep to face the rigors of Sunday, when I was awakened by the unsettling ring of the phone. The caller was a man in our church. With urgency in his voice, he told of a head-on collision that had just taken place up the road from his home. A drunk driver, passing, had met head-on an oncoming car at the top of a rise. The car with the DWI driver slid into the ditch in flames, leaving the three occupants of the other car seriously injured. The caller went on to tell me that he thought the people in that car were from our church. He mentioned their names. I knew immediately who they were.

Dave had attended college with me and was now an attorney with a blossoming law practice. Debbie was a homemaker whose life had become enriched with the birth of a son. Sean was the third occupant of the car.

The caller went on to say that the ambulance had already taken all three to the hospital. I hung up quickly and called the emergency room. Had they been admitted? Yes, they had, the nurse told me. Their condition? She wasn't allowed to give that information over the phone. But I was their pastor. "If you're their pastor you should come as soon as possible."

As I hurried into the emergency room, I walked past the first cubicle where my college friend lay unattended, unconscious. In the next cubicle, a doctor and several nurses were working feverishly over the body of their precious son. Then, from across the room, I heard someone calling.

"Pastor, Pastor!" It was Debbie. Though conscious, her face had been torn by the impact of the crash. I stood next to her and spoke with her for a brief moment. We prayed together. As I turned around to walk back to Dave, I saw the nurses pull the curtains around the child and leave him alone. He had slipped on to be with his Father in heaven.

Dave's and Debbie's injuries were so serious that they were transferred by ambulance to a larger hospital, where Debbie underwent several hours of extensive surgery while Dave remained unconscious. Debbie's parents asked if I would please stay through the night and wait for Debbie to wake up from the anesthetic. They were sure she would ask about Sean, and they felt I should tell her.

I sat through that night wondering what I would say. What could I say? I didn't know the why of what happened. I still don't. Neither do they. All I could do was turn her heart toward that which was certain and true.

As morning came, our church service started several miles away. For all those at church it was another Sunday, another day like every other day. But for Dave and Debbie everything had changed, and it would never be the same. Without notice or warning their existence had been intercepted by tragedy. It was as though they had suddenly been placed into a separate sphere of existence. All around them the rush and routine of the masses living their lives to the beat of all that is normal went on without interruption, but they were no longer a part of that. Dave, Debbie, and those of us with them were struggling with issues of life at their deepest and most profound level.

What I felt through that night and what Dave and Debbie would wrestle with in the days and months ahead was that hellish tension between feelings of anger and betrayal and the felt need to throw ourselves humbly at His feet, pleading for mercy and grace to help.

I knew that the words I would say would point the arrows in the right or wrong direction. Toward the growth and glory that God could bring through the tragedy or toward the destruction and ruin Satan had in mind. Whatever the words would be, they needed to lift their hearts and minds toward Him, their only hope for healing.

I prayed for wisdom.

THE TROUBLE WITH LIFE

Growing up in a pastor's home, I remember falling asleep at night to the sound of my parents working in our living room with people whose lives had experienced that "great fall." People who somehow hoped that my father would be better than "all the king's horses and all the king's men" at putting the pieces of their lives back together again. I remember the sobs of the alcoholic who was back on a binge after having lost his family and a successful career.

The first sermon I preached was in a New York City mission. I doubt if I will ever forget the impact of sitting on the platform and looking out over that sea of glazed faces, knowing that at one time their lives had been full of dreams, their marriages filled with hope and expectation, their careers on the upward track. Now life had taken a tragic turn and their lives were empty of resolve, void of dignity, and depleted of hope. Mere existence.

Following in my father's footsteps, I was off to seminary where I was exposed to four years of in-depth study of theology, biblical data, and ministry theory and skills. Within the first few months of landing in the pastorate, a young wife and mother came to see me after a service, wanting to know if she could stop by during the week. The appointment was set. She arrived, sat down, and proceeded to tell me she no longer loved her husband. There was no one else, she did not want to leave her husband for the children's sake, and she did not want to feel this way about her husband. She told me that many of their friends seemed to have happy and fulfilling relationships with each other and it was her goal to somehow reclaim those lost feelings that had at one time held so much hope for fulfillment and happiness. I scrambled for something meaningful to say.

All of life runs unsettlingly close to the ditch.

That was the beginning of my regular exposure to the tyranny of trouble in people's lives. Hours of ministry were filled with standing by people like Martha who, married to one of my close friends from high school, only weeks after she and her husband began their life's work as a missionary couple watched her husband and my friend die a slow and agonizing death. I've walked with men through the ego-wrenching pain of job loss and marketplace failure. I've listened to the probing questions of the widow, who after years of sacrificing her husband's presence to ministry, stood with great anticipation on the threshold of retirement and life together at the North Carolina hideaway only to have his life taken in a plane crash over the chilled Alaskan ocean, never to be seen again. What hope can there be for a young wife and mother who has discovered explicitly sensual love notes passed between her husband and their high school baby-sitter detailing nights away at a motel in a nearby town?

I've watched trouble compound itself into networks of complexity, weaving chains of despondency and despair around extended families, friends, and ensuing generations. Untangling those networks often brought to ruin through abuse and addiction seems at times an impossible task.

All of life runs unsettlingly close to the ditch. Trouble is indiscriminate in its timing and its choice of target. Job, who bore the scars to validate his wisdom, said, "Man is born to trouble as surely as sparks fly upward" (Job 5:7). In fact, the entire landscape of our existence is vulnerable. From health, to emotions, mind, finances, marketplace, family, and friends—trouble stands at the brink of it all, waiting to make its unwelcome, untimely, usually unexpected entrance.

No one is exempt.

No arena of life is out of bounds.

So pervasive a reality is trouble that even Dr. Seuss warns children of the inevitable downside of life. He writes,

> You'll be on your way up!
> You'll be seeing great sights!
> You'll join the high flyers who soar
> to great heights.

> You won't lag behind, because you'll
> have the speed.
> You'll pass the whole gang and you'll soon
> take the lead.
> Where ever you fly, you'll be the best of the best.
> Where ever you go, you will top all the rest.

> Except when you *don't*
> Because, sometimes, you *won't.*

> I'm sorry to say so
> But, sadly, it's true
> That bang-ups
> And hang-ups
> *Can* happen to you.

> You can get all hung-up
> In a prickle-ly perch.
> And your gang will fly on.
> You'll be left in a lurch.

You'll come down from the lurch
With an unpleasant bump.
And the chances are, then,
That you'll be in a slump.

And when you're in a slump,
You're not in for much fun.
Unslumping yourself is not easily done.[1]

Given the inevitability of trouble, it's no surprise that we spend great amounts of time, energy, and money trying to unslump ourselves. Counselors, psychologists, and psychiatrists are in abundant supply. Group therapy sessions are crowded. Support groups for nearly every affliction imaginable are available, and are present even in some of our churches. Groups for addiction, abuse, stress, grief, and overeating offer hope in unslumping ourselves. There is even a group called Super Moms Anonymous, whose sole purpose is to give support and relief to women who are trying to deal with the stress of trying to combine a career, a husband, and raising a family.

Nevertheless, it is true that help and healing begin and end in all that He is and all that He provides.

Big-ticket seminars offer hope. Meditation says you can unslump yourself by getting in touch with yourself, and health clubs offer exercise programs and group activities to make life with all of its troubles more tolerable and meaningful.

1. From *Oh, the Places You'll Go!* by Dr. Seuss. Copyright © 1990 by Theodor S. Geisel and Audrey S. Geisel. Reprinted by permission of Random House, Inc.

Many of the alternatives compound our problems. Alcohol, drugs, the unbridled pursuit of sensual pleasure, and the consuming passion to accumulate things, status, power, and prestige offer themselves as elusive remedies; cruises and exotic vacations are advertised "escape weekends"—but our trouble still goes with us.

We laugh on the outside while we're crying on the inside. We often feel lonely in a crowd.

Ultimately, we end up wondering if there is any genuine, enduring hope when we hurt.

Grinning and bearing it offers resolve but no solution. Getting mad only tends to bring more grief and anguish as we walk through life like a fight looking for a place to happen. Getting even starts wars that escalate and sap our resources, as bitterness eats away at our souls. Withdrawal creates additional conflict as we end up living in a ghetto of one, watching from the sidelines as the rest of the world races by.

Is There Any Hope?

Though there are rarely simple solutions and never lasting quick fixes for our troubles, there are realities that produce hope and healing in the midst of hurt.

When trouble invades our comfort zones two needs rise to the top: the need for *understanding* (to find answers to the probing and disturbing questions that crowd our minds and souls) and the need for *healing* (to feel better and to finish the problem). Of the two, understanding is the key to effectively managing the problem to its ultimate outcome. Without the understanding that produces the right answers there is no sense of direction and no hope in which to feel secure.

The right answers begin by asking the right questions. And the right question is not, "Why?" Though it is no doubt our first question in the midst of pain, it is not the most strategic question. For that we can be thankful. Attempts to resolve hurt by seeking specific personal answers to the question, "Why?" usually compound our problems rather than solve them, since there are rarely adequate answers.

Being preoccupied in the "Why" syndrome may even create a downward cycle of despair that is tough to recover from. You know you are on the wrong track when all you can think of is:

Why me?
Why me again?
Why now?
Why did this have to happen?
Why did God not stop it?
Is there something wrong with me?
Is there something wrong with Him?
Is there something I've missed about life?
Why are others seemingly free from trouble?
Why don't people understand?
Why don't people care?
Why don't they get their act together?
Why do I keep blowing it?
Why do I keep living?

Processing problems in the "why zone" too often leaves us cynical, hardened, angry, and confused. The only right answer to "Why?" is "I don't know why—and if I don't know why, I need to suspend judgment until I do."

Job's devastating experience is helpful at this point. Only a brief part of his story deals with recounting his problems. The bulk of the material in the book of Job focuses on the advice of his wife and friends, who try to answer the question, "Why?" and who counsel him from that perspective. Their efforts only compound his problem. In the end God resolves the mental anguish by turning Job from the question, "Why?" to the question, "Who?"

Hope begins when we start with the right question, "Who?"

The answer to "Who?" is threefold.

Him—God our Father in all His supreme authority, presence, and power.

Me—target of the trouble and in sole control of my responses and actions.

Them—the people around me who may have caused the pain, who awkwardly try to help me in my pain, and who don't understand, sometimes don't even care.

We must immediately get the "them" in perspective. Since we can't control them we are not wise to focus on them or expect much from them. If God sees fit to use some of "them" to provide hope, then let it be an added blessing.

That leaves two points of focus.

Him and *me.*

In the first episode of the "Star Wars" trilogy, Princess Leia, captured by the evil forces of the universe and helpless to improve her condition, logs a laser beam message into the computer chip reservoir of the android R2D2. The message is directed to the only one who can help her, Obi-Wan Kenobi. He is the last vestige of that which is moral, just, and good in the universe. The message urgently pleads, "Help me Obi-Wan Kenobi. You're my only hope."

Captured by forces beyond ourselves and locked into circumstances beyond our control, we log prayer messages, hoping that they will be heard by the Eternal God, who is the only true and reliable source of all that is moral, just, and good in the universe.

No doubt it sounds simplistic, and to some is even unwelcome, to say that ultimately God is our only hope. Nevertheless, it is true that help and healing begin and end in all that He is and all that He provides. That is not to say that He does not work through pastors, wise biblical counselors, friends, sermons, books, groups, the study of His Word, experience, circumstances, or prayer. Nor is it to say that healing cannot be sudden or that it may be slow or even that some pain may be permanent, requiring a special adjustment that is both victorious and fulfilling. It is simply to affirm that our hope and eventual healing begin by looking in His direction. Through the work of the Spirit, and according to the principles and power of His Word, ultimately He is the genuine helper and healer. Without Him, help is at best cosmetic, incomplete, temporary, and sometimes misguided.

When Scripture speaks of hope it literally means to trust in a present and future help that is *certain*. Our English word for hope lacks this element of certainty. I could say every day for a year, "I *hope* this problem is gone by tomorrow morning," and each morning accurately express the English sense of "hope." It is little more than a wish. A "hope so." It does not need to be grounded in a certain reality.

Biblical hope is grounded in *certainty*. The only certain, steady reality when life takes a downward turn is our Father in heaven and the helping work of His Spirit through the guiding principles of His Word. God is full of certainties that provide something solid to hope in. Those certainties are like handles to which we cling. They are exclamation points amid the nagging question marks. God is not slippery or inaccessible. He is more than a mystical, ethereal notion. He is more than mere mental theological truth. He is real. Really there. Really here. In all His compassionate power He cannot be anything but what He is. Nor does He hoard His resources. He shares them. In time. In abundance. In wisdom and strength. He is more than words. He is wonder and power.

When we begin with "who," we begin with Him. It may only be a determined resolve to look trustingly in His direction. It may be unsophisticated. But it must begin with Him.

For some, hope in God will seem to conflict with thoughts of His distance and the damage He has permitted in our lives. However, if we are willing to open our hearts and minds, we will come to know how, when, and the ways in which His certainties can become realities that bring hope and eventual healing.

With the psalmist we can come to enjoy the confidence of proclaiming,

> The Lord is my light and my salvation;
> Whom shall I fear?
> The Lord is the defense of my life;
> Whom shall I dread?
> When evildoers came upon me to devour my flesh,
> My adversaries and my enemies
>   they stumbled and fell.
> Though a host encamp against me,
> My heart will not fear;
> Though war rise against me,
> In spite of this I shall be confident.
>
> One thing I have asked from the Lord,
>   that I shall seek:
> That I may dwell in the house of the Lord
>   all the days of my life,
> To behold the beauty of the Lord,
> And to meditate in His temple.
> For in the day of trouble He will
>   conceal me in His tabernacle;
> In the secret place of His tent
>   He will hide me;
> He will lift me up on a rock.
> And now my head will be lifted up
>   above my enemies around me;

And I will offer in His tent
    sacrifices with shouts of joy;
I will sing, yes, I will sing praises
    to the Lord.

Hear, O Lord, when I cry with my voice,
And be gracious to me and answer me.
When Thou didst say, "Seek My face,"
    my heart said to Thee,
"Thy face, O Lord, I shall seek."
                (Psalm 27:1-8, NASB*)

and to finally rejoice,

I waited patiently for the Lord;
    he turned to me and heard my cry.
He lifted me out of the slimy pit,
    out of the mud and mire;
he set my feet on a rock
    and gave me a firm place to stand.
He put a new song in my mouth,
    a hymn of praise to our God.
Many will see and fear
    and put their trust in the Lord.
                (Psalm 40:1-5)

THE OTHER SIDE OF WHO

The other side of "Who?" is "me." Me—with all my feelings, hurts, confusion, and questions.

In trouble, the most strategic part of me is my *will*. It remains intact in spite of loose ends around me and my jumbled emotions. Our wills are the only entities we control and the only point of certain relationship with Him.

Often, despair in pain is deepened by the thought that there is nothing we can do about our situation, that

New American Standard Bible.

we are victimized by overwhelming and uncontrollable circumstances. Our every effort to protect ourselves from husband, wife, child, or parent, our every effort to correct failing health or reverse financial loss has been frustrated. What do we do when there is nothing left to do, when life is out of control?

What do we do when even our trust in God seems shaky? When answers are not immediate and God seems far away? When we do not know how to tap His help and are left to wait passively for Him to answer, wishing for some spectacular flurry of divine activity to deliver us? What are we to do when that rescue doesn't come, and unfulfilled expectations for help from Him turn our hearts toward doubt? When we begin to slip back to the "Whys?"—Why me? Why not them? Why now?—and tend to doubt His goodness and may even doubt that He actually does love and care for us.

Perhaps we will doubt that we are worthy of His concern. Increasingly we may even feel that there is no hope for us in God. And, when we begin to believe that for us He is not there and He does not care, we cross a threshold of vulnerability to the debilitating forces of anger and cynicism that bring us further distress and eventual defeat.

We can look downward in despair.
. . . Or we can look upward to Him.

Before that happens, we must turn to the entity over which we exercise exclusive control, our *wills,* to the choices we have to think correctly and respond constructively.

My thoughts, my responses, and my decisions are always within my jurisdiction in the midst of trouble. I can choose to keep looking to Him even when all is quiet in the sky. I am in charge of my choice to seek forgiveness when I have failed and to forgive others when they have failed, to persevere in correct and productive responses, to love or hate, resent and seek revenge. The old song that declares "It's not my brother or my sister but it's me, O Lord, standing in the need of prayer" strikes at the heart of it all.

It is no coincidence that when Scripture speaks to the context of trouble it never wallows in the despair of our hopeless circumstances but always guides us to the Lord and then specifically prescribes achievable options that we *by choice* either embrace or reject.

If we are to find hope and help when it hurts, we must begin with the "who" of it all. We must hope in the certainty of what is true about God and then be committed to control the "me" so that within the context of what the Lord prescribes we can respond correctly and constructively to our situation.

Though we often view trouble as an issue of "me" versus "my circumstances," in reality hope dawns when we refocus our thinking and view our situation as a matter of constructively and biblically controlling the "me" and trusting the truth about "Him"—the One who controls my circumstances.

If we choose not to cultivate our hope in Him, where will we place our hope? Is there anything greater, more just, more equitable, more powerful, more reliable, more true than God? Or are we children of lesser gods? Will we hope in the gods of comfort, peace, pleasure, and self-fulfillment? Will we deify ourselves to be the ultimate helper and healer through clever, manipulative, vindictive, or even well-intended schemes? Or will we be children of the true and living God, who is indeed our ultimate and final hope when we are overwhelmed?

Healing begins with a choice to place our hope in Him. The process continues as we choose to cultivate and commit ourselves unconditionally to those certainties and principles of response that are anchored in the bedrock of what we know to be true and sure regardless of how we feel or how difficult the circumstances around us.

It is an issue of where we look. We can look downward in despair and outward in fear and confusion as we survey our circumstances. Or we can look upward to Him and inward to our choices.

Sometimes, however, hope in God may be threatened by the haunting sense that He is the One to blame for all our troubles. Since He is a God who is all-powerful and sovereignly aware of every moment and movement on this planet, could not He have prevented what happened and granted us an exemption from trauma, as He seems to have done for others?

Is He to blame?

Could a loving God, who says He is concerned for us, ever have a reason to let us experience such trauma? Until we understand His place in our problem, hoping in Him will be a tough assignment.

2

Who's to Blame?

The Source and Resolution
of Difficulty

The transatlantic connection was weak and filled with static, but the reality of a broken heart on the other end of the line was clear. It was Martie, Craig's wife. As she spoke, everything inside me felt crushed.

Craig and I grew up together. After attending the same college, I went off to seminary. Craig married Martie, a pretty coed in his class, and enlisted in the Air Force.

We lost touch.

Our paths merged again a few years later as I assumed my first pastorate. It soon became apparent that our lifestyles had taken two divergent tracks. Craig had lost interest in the Lord, and he and Martie lived in the fast lane. Yet, in time, God began to work in their lives. They reconciled themselves to Christ and became active in our small fellowship of believers.

Craig taught our high school boys, and Martie taught the girls. It was a great joy to see Craig and Martie give

their lives completely to Christ for whatever He wanted
them to do. In time that led them to answer God's call
to work with troubled teens on the island of Haiti. They
were the first missionaries to go out from our blossoming work. There was a tremendous sense of fulfillment
as we commissioned them to their work for Christ on
the island of Haiti.

They'd been in Haiti only a week—and now Martie
was telling me that Craig had suffered a severe injury
while diving into a pool. He had been taken in a jeep
across the rugged trail to a primitive hospital where he
lay with a broken neck. His head and face, she said,
were swollen beyond recognition. Craig didn't make it
through the night. Martie was there alone. A widow.

It made no sense to me. My mind was filled with
questions that had no answers. I felt despondency and
defeat. *Why, God? Why now? Why them?* Somehow,
way down inside, Craig's death clashed with my belief
that God was wise, all-powerful, and loving.

THE TROUBLE WITH TROUBLE

The trouble with trouble is that it threatens not
just our comfort and peace but our faith in God. Pain so
conflicts with our concept of what we expect God to be
like that trying to merge our pain with His claims is almost too risky to attempt head-on. It is easier to retreat
into pious-sounding statements and hide under hollow
phrases that have little meaning and no healing value
or, more damaging, embitter our hearts and cause us to
withdraw our spirits from Him.

We must take the risk to understand God and the
role He plays in pain. There is no hope until we understand the way God interfaces with problems, what He
supplies in the process, and what He seeks to accomplish. Viewing our trouble from the vantage point of
truth about God equips us to make it through a crisis

with hands held high in victory. Getting a handle on how God relates to trouble will help us in tough times and will equip us to encourage, guide, and comfort others as we walk with them through deep waters.

REJECTING WHAT IS NOT TRUE

Unfortunately, it is sometimes difficult to see God's place in our problems because a clear view of His role is often obscured by myths. If we respond to our difficulty in the context of those myths, our problems will only compound themselves. There are at least five prevalent, though false, perceptions about the problem of pain and God's role in the midst of it.

For those of us who have come to the cross and received . . . cleansing for our sin, difficulty is never punishment.

Pain is punishment. When our lives are impacted by difficulty, our minds tend to race through the history of our existence to find out "why I'm being punished like this." We review our lives to see if some failure will explain our pain.

Though it is true that God does discipline us with difficulty (Proverbs 3; Hebrews 12), it is also true that not all difficulty is discipline. And for the believer, none of it is punishment. For those of us who have come to the cross and received full past, present, and future cleansing for our sin, difficulty is never punishment. All of our sins have been punished in Jesus Christ through His work on the cross. Discipline is different. Unlike punishment, it is intended to nudge us back to righteous living. And though some pain may also be the consequence of sin, God promises that even in the worst cases there is potential for glory and gain.

Christ's disciples were evidently locked into the "pain is punishment" mind-set. In passing by the beggar born blind they asked, "Rabbi, who sinned, this man or his parents, that he was born blind?" (John 9:2) It was as though they thought punishment was the only reason for pain. Christ's response was interesting: "Neither this man nor his parents sinned, but this happened so that the work of God might be displayed in his life" (v. 3). The beggar's pain had nothing to do with punishment for sin, discipline, or the consequence of wrong choices. The tragedy in his life was a stage upon which Christ was to demonstrate His power and glory. Christ would touch his eyes and he would see, and through his trouble God's authority and power would become evident.

Responding well to trauma
demands that we . . . look to see
what is true about the role God
plays in the process.

Pain is unproductive. In our addiction to pleasure, peace, comfort, and ease, we see trouble as a nonproductive interruption. Yet pain is indeed productive. It brings us to a clear sense of ourselves and it clarifies our values. When tragedy strikes, all that is fleeting and temporary, all that we had wrongly valued so highly, is quickly relegated to its rightful position. Trouble brings God, family, friends, and our inner strengths and weaknesses into sharp focus. The consistent message of Scripture is that trouble is not intended to break us but to make us. It is not to make us bitter but to make us better.

In God's hand there is always gain in pain. Indeed, Romans 5:3-5 asserts that trauma can be productive: "We also rejoice in our sufferings, because we know that suffering produces perseverance; perseverance, character; and character, hope. And hope does not disappoint us, because God has poured out his love into our hearts by the Holy Spirit, whom he has given us." James underscores the point by affirming that trouble serves to make us "mature and complete, not lacking anything" (James 1:4).

Pain is indicative of spiritual failure. It is easy to assume that the "good life" is a sign of God's blessing. We are told that if we have plenty of faith, we can be happy, healthy, and wealthy. In this context, trouble becomes a reflection of a less-than-productive faith and thus a bad reflection on our spiritual standing. In the face of this misunderstanding, Scripture makes clear that some of God's most faithful and mature people have suffered ill health, trouble, and trauma of all kinds (2 Corinthians 12:7-10; Philippians 2:25-27; 1 Timothy 5:23; 1 Peter 2:21-24). Hebrews 11:35b-38 catalogs the trouble of God's finest when it states:

> Others were tortured and refused to be released, so that they might gain a better resurrection. Some faced jeers and flogging, while still others were chained and put in prison. They were stoned; they were sawed in two; they were put to death by the sword. They went about in sheepskins and goatskins, destitute, persecuted and mistreated—the world was not worthy of them. They wandered in deserts and mountains, and in caves and holes in the ground.

Heroes of the faith are not exempt from trouble.

Pain is not good. Scripture affirms, "And we know that in all things God works for the good of those who love Him, who have been called according to his purpose" (Romans 8:28). God affirms in this text that pain is equated with that which is good. We are quick to define good only in terms of comfort, convenience, and prosperity, but God indicates that pain is a means to achieving ultimate good. That does not discount the unsettling and troubling reality of our suffering, but it does enable us to recognize that in the big picture, pain is a part of a process that can ultimately come to that which is good.

Pain is incompatible with a God who is good and all-powerful. In his best-seller *When Bad Things Happen to Good People,* Harold Kushner writes: "The misfortunes of good people are not only a problem to the people who suffer and to their families, they are a problem to everyone who wants to believe in a just and fair and livable world. They inevitably raise questions about the goodness, the kindness, even the existence of God."[1]

Although this may well be the most prevalent misconception about pain, the truth is that God's goodness and power are not in contradiction to the presence of difficulty but are instead the very realities that offer hope and a solution in the midst of pain.

Responding well to trauma demands that we dismiss wrong conclusions about our problems and look to see what is true about the role God plays in the process.

WHO'S TO BLAME?

In the beginning, God created an environment that was painless and trouble free. All of creation was a reflection of God's magnificent glory. Human life existed in unhindered fulfillment and unbridled joy through a delightful and harmonious relationship to the Creator and the perfect created world.

1. Harold S. Kushner, *When Bad Things Happen to Good People* (New York: Schocken, 1981, pp. 6-7.

From the stars in the heavens to man himself, the *primary purpose* of creation was to demonstrate in visible fashion the limitless glory of God's character and capacities (see Genesis 1:26-27; Psalm 19:1).

At the center of this exhibit of God's glory was man and the element of choice God gave to man. Adam and Eve were not created as robots but rather were created with the capacity to choose to obey and worship God (Genesis 2:15-17). Their choice to obey and worship would be a dramatic statement that God in and of Himself was worthy of a man's glad and uncompromised allegiance. If God had not given man the option to choose, not only would man's expressions of love to God be meaningless, but God's worth and value could not be truly expressed.

There was no sorrow until Satan and sin appeared on the landscape.

Yet an integral part of that free choice was the potential to choose not to obey and worship God. And that is exactly what happened (Genesis 3:1-6). Adam and Eve elected not to obey God, and the entrance of sin made its presence felt by the impact of the consequences of sin. God's original intent in creation was the provision of a painless environment, a world free of pain or trouble, but when mankind chose to take the wonderful freedom God had given him to willfully express love and allegiance to Him and turned that freedom selfward to be consumed on self-directed fulfillment, the door was open to pain, and pain became the natural expression of sin's residence in the history and experience of mankind.

This longing for self-oriented fulfillment is today a source of much pain and suffering. Independence from

God's plan and an allegiance to self-determination opens the door to trouble every time.

The source of trouble is best understood on two levels. On the surface, man took the privilege of free will and prostituted it on the altar of self-serving desires (Genesis 3:6). The divine arrangement for freedom of choice obviously held within it the potential for failure. The failure, however, was ours. God was no more responsible for this failure than a teacher who gives a test in which there is potential for a student to fail. We, mankind, made the choice to sin.

That choice changed everything.

On the second level, we must understand that when Adam and Eve transferred their loyalty to Satan, they enabled Satan to establish himself as the dominant force in this world (2 Corinthians 4:4). Since Adam and Eve were assigned to be the governors of all creation (Genesis 1:26), Satan was enabled to invade into creation through them and to gain control of it by controlling them. As Paul stated so clearly, all of us and all of creation now groan under the curse of sin (Romans 8:18-23). Sin is the source of pain, and Satan is the source of sin.

Now the blame becomes lodged in proper quarters.

There was no sorrow until Satan and sin appeared on the landscape. As soon as sin hit the scene, it brought death, as God had warned it would. Death with all of its trouble and trauma. There was not only physical death, but there was the death of self-esteem (Genesis 3:7), the intrusion of personal shame and alienation (Genesis 3:8), the presence of anxiety and fear (Genesis 3:10), and the weight of guilt and subsequent attempts to transfer responsibility to others (Genesis 3:12). There was pain even in the pinnacle experience of life, childbirth (Genesis 3:16). The fulfillment of productive labor turned into toil and weeds, thistles and exhaustion (Genesis 3:17-19). By the close of Genesis 4, Adam and Eve had seen jealousy, anger, and murder, experienced the pain of losing a child, and witnessed the increase of violence in the establishment of a godless environment—all of it the agony of the consequence of sin.

GOD'S RESPONSE

God could have annihilated everything right then. Yet He chose instead to take Satan's finest efforts to deface His glory and turn them into *glory* and *gain* for those who would yield to His process in the midst of their trouble and pain. Ultimately, that would mean His own suffering and shame as He stepped into this fallen world to experience trouble and death to undo the personal penalty of sin for all who will trust Him. No, God is not the immediate source of pain. Yet He remains the ultimate solution to all that is bad and horrible in this world.

It should not go unnoticed that when God speaks to us about the problem of pain, He consistently defines its source in terms of Satan's influence and the debilitating effects of the reality of sin. All of Job's suffering was at the hand of Satan (Job 1, 2). Paul's thorn in the flesh was a messenger of Satan (2 Corinthians 12:7). The weaknesses of our bodies are a result of the curse of sin (Romans 8:23). Trouble and trauma are the natural byproducts of the presence of sin (Genesis 3, 4).

It is a gauge of how greatly sin has distorted our thinking when we realize that Satan has turned our minds from blaming him to blaming God for our troubles, as though they were all His fault. God doesn't deserve the blame. Recognizing this truth is the first step toward coming to Him when it hurts, to the One who is our only hope.

The struggle about God's place in pain is not completely resolved by simply affirming that He is not the source of our trouble. No doubt some of us are willing to accept this truth—and yet our hearts cry, *If He is all-powerful, why doesn't He stop my pain?* In fact, God does stop much if not most pain and suffering from ever getting to us in the first place. If it weren't for His guardianship at the gates of our existence, we would be consumed. What God does permit Satan to inflict is subject to God's capacity to bring about glory and gain through it all. The wonder of it all is that God takes Satan's finest efforts to deface God's reputation and turns them completely to His glory!

How does that happen? It is *our response* to pain that is crucial to the process. For those of us who love God and His cause it is a high motivation to deal constructively with trouble, not for our sakes alone but for His glory before a watching world.

SATAN'S STRATEGIC PURPOSE IN PAIN

Understanding Satan's use of pain as a strategic assault upon the dignity of God is vital in helping us cultivate a constructive response to pain. Satan uses trouble to defame the glory of God. All of creation—and that includes us and everything and everyone around us—was created to bring glory to God. God intended that we should be living statements that accurately, visibly reflect the strength of His magnificent quality and character. Pain and trouble are Satan's graffiti scrawled across the face of God's glory. They are Satan's way of getting back at God, of staining God's reputation.

Commuting to work, I watched day by day as a beautiful office building rose out of the ground. In front was a large sign with a picture of the completed project. Under the picture, proudly stated, were the names of the the architect and the contractor. This building was to be a clear reflection of their capacity to design and build a magnificent structure. It would be their glory.

One night, when the building was nearly completed, vandals defaced the building with spray paint. It was an ugly scene. The beauty of the building was marred and its glory stained.

That is Satan's purpose in pain.

Unfortunately, Satan has been quite successful in his strategic attack. When was the last time we heard Satan and sin blamed for war, blight, starvation, or crime? Who usually gets blamed for murder, rape, greed, trauma, trouble, or difficulty? Mostly the blame is unfairly laid at the feet of God.

Satan does not care about us or our environment. He only seeks to use us and abuse us as tools to carry out his revenge against God. Satan once desired God's glory for himself and was denied (Isaiah 14:12-17). He now seeks to destroy the glory that is God's alone, the glory that he could not have. It's as though he says, "If I can't have it, God will not have it either."

Given Satan's firm hold on this planet and the impact of sin's presence, we must remember continually that we live in a fallen place in the midst of a fallen race. Not one of us is exempt from pain. Jesus wept (John 11:35). Timothy needed some wine for his stomach's sake (1 Timothy 5:23). Epaphroditus was sick unto death (Philippians 2:27). Paul lived with a thorn in his flesh (1 Corinthians 12:7-10). Trophimus was left at Miletus sick (2 Timothy 4:20). The apostles were martyred. First-century Christians were burned at the stake, and some were fed to lions. In a sin-bound system, trouble is certain. No one is exempt, not even the best of us. We must not let trouble surprise us.

That only plays into Satan's scheme and opens the doors of our hearts to the destructive forces of bitterness and further pain. Our response to pain should not be to blame God. We should rather flee to Him as our only hope, seeking to cooperate with His principles so that His sustaining grace and overcoming power might reverse the intent of Satan and grant us the privilege of bringing glory to God in the midst of Satan's strategic assault on God's character.

Since God's agenda is to use sin-imposed trouble to create glory and gain, we should be careful not to impose our dreams, timetables, and particular agendas on Him. All too often we are tempted to cooperate on our terms for our own purposes. Yielding to Him truly *means* yielding to Him—yielding to His timing, His will, His way, His purpose.

WHAT CAN WE EXPECT?

We can expect some solid things from God to help us in the process.

To find hope when it hurts,
. . . start by affirming that
God is not to be blamed, but
to be trusted and obeyed.

The first thing we can expect is to feel secure in His assured victory over sin, death, pain, and trouble. My trouble today is wrapped in a broader conflict that began deep in the past and stretches far into the future. In the future a day will come when He will "wipe away every tear" and "there will be no death or mourning or crying or pain, for the old order of things has passed away," for He said, "I am making everything new" (Revelation 21:4-5). The eradication of trouble will be permanent and eternal. We will be safely restored to the ecstasy of Eden, this time unable to fail.

The future assurance in and of itself brings hope. No matter how tough it gets, "this too shall pass." Today's problems will pale in the perspective of our eternal liberation from the tyranny of this earthbound experience.

This future assurance is grounded in history. The past holds our guarantee for a better tomorrow. In the *past* Christ came to deal a fatal blow to sin and its power over us. Isaiah 53:4-7 prophetically declares:

> Surely he took up our infirmities
> and carried our sorrows,
> yet we considered him stricken by God,
> smitten by him and afflicted.
> But he was pierced for our transgressions,
> he was crushed for our iniquities;
> the punishment that brought us peace was upon him,
> and by his wounds we are healed.
> We all, like sheep, have gone astray,
> each one of us has turned to his own way;
> and the Lord has laid on him
> the iniquity of us all.
>
> He was oppressed and afflicted
> yet he did not open his mouth;
> he was led like a lamb to the slaughter,
> and as a sheep before her shearers is silent
> so he did not open his mouth.

Believers have a past certainty sealed in the historical fact of the cross and the resurrection. Because of the resurrection, we are assured of the future. Paul wrote at the conclusion of his defense of the resurrection:

> Listen, I tell you a mystery. We will not all sleep, but we will all be changed—in a flash, in the twinkling of an eye, at the last trumpet. For the trumpet will sound, the dead will be raised imperishable, and we will be changed. For the perishable must clothe itself with the imperishable, and the mortal with immortality. When the perishable has been clothed with the imperishable,

and the mortal with immortality, then the saying that is written will come true: "Death has been swallowed up in victory."

"Where O death, is your victory?
Where, O death, is your sting?"

The sting of death is sin, and the power of sin is the law. But thanks be to God! He gives us the victory through our Lord Jesus Christ.

Therefore, my dear brothers, stand firm. Let nothing move you. Always give yourselves fully to the work of the Lord, because you know that your labor in the Lord is not in vain. (1 Corinthians 15:52-58)

Like no other system of belief, Christianity has a clear and present identity with the problem of pain. At the center of it all is a cruel instrument of torture. In fact, the cross stands as the symbol of our faith the world around. When the eternal God decided to come to our planet to rescue this world from the stranglehold of sin, He did not send legions of armed angels to obliterate Satan and his host. He came Himself. All alone in the Person of Jesus Christ. And though He had every right to establish a royal presence as the sovereign ruler of the universe, demanding that people pay homage to Him, He came instead as a suffering Savior, "a man of sorrows, and acquainted with grief." He knew what it was to be despised and rejected of men. He tasted loneliness. He was misunderstood, misrepresented, and often maligned. He knew moments of fame and the roar of the crowd, and He knew the fickle defection of the masses. When they should have been proclaiming Him King of kings, they cried, "Crucify Him!" Worse, they called for the release of the criminal Barabbas that they might have His blood. When it was time for Him to die, He died not in the dignity He deserved but in injustice and dishonor.

God is not a spectator when it comes to pain. He has been willing to be a participant that He might now reign as our empathic High Priest who has walked the road before us. As the writer of Hebrews states,

> Since we have a great high priest who has gone through the heavens, Jesus the Son of God, let us hold firmly to the faith we profess. For we do not have a high priest who is unable to sympathize with our weaknesses, but we have one who has been tempted in every way, just as we are—yet was without sin. Let us then approach the throne of grace with confidence, so that we may receive mercy and find grace to help us in our time of need. (Hebrews 4:14-16)

Which brings us to *now.* Too often Christianity seems anchored in history and focused on the future as though there were little relevance to the present. I'm reminded of the queen in Lewis Carroll's *Through the Looking Glass.* She complained, "Jam tomorrow and jam yesterday—but never jam today." But God does provide certainties of significance today—in the midst of our pain.

GRACE, GROWTH, AND GLORY

The Scripture speaks of at least three of those certainties: grace, growth, and glory. The grace is His power to sustain us regardless (2 Corinthians 12:9). The growth is the development of our personhood in both character and competency (Romans 5:3-5; James 1:1-5). The glory is the reflection of His character and capacity through our suffering as the world watches to see if our God is powerful enough and good enough to be counted on in trouble (John 9:3-4).

If we are to find hope when it hurts, we start by affirming that God is not to be blamed, but to be trusted and obeyed as He brings us through it all with an outpouring of His grace for our growth and the ultimate gain of glory.

I had served together with Doug and Doreen and had seen often their clear commitment to the cause of Jesus Christ. We had waited through the nine months and then rejoiced in the birth of their precious baby boy, only now to receive a call reporting that their baby had died in its crib. Revived by the emergency squad, he lived on mechanical support for three days. We spent hours together in the hospital. Through their tears and confusion, Doug and Doreen portrayed an unusual and unique strength in it all. So unusual was this response that the hospital staff, who no doubt had seen many parents in the same conflict, observed to the Olsens, "You must be religious."

As the hours passed, the medical staff began to recognize something deeper than religion. Before the ordeal was over, they had asked about the faith that had so evidently strengthened this couple in the midst of their pain. The answer was clear. It was their unshakable faith in the sovereign plan and purpose of their all-wise and loving God regardless of the earthly outcome. It was the sufficiency of God's grace that provided the platform for His glory. Though Doug and Doreen still don't know the "Why?," they have grown in character and competency.

The grace, growth, and glory of God do not make trouble any less painful, but they do fill pain with strength, confidence, and purpose. Grace and glory are the realities of God's provision that enable us to overcome. Glory to Him is the ultimate result. In Christ, temporary loss is always in the context of ultimate gain. Overcomers reach for the grace, yield to the growth, and anticipate the glory.

A few months after Craig's death, Martie wrote:

> Thank You, Lord, for choosing me
>   to view Your pain at Calvary.
> Your tearstained paths of grief You share
>   with me these days because You care.
> Thank You for the time I cried
>   within the garden, by Your side,
> "If it be possible for Thee,
>   please, God, this cup remove from Me.
> Thank You, too, for the burden I bear
>   for the loneliness, and for the despair,
> For beneath this cross, and on this road
>   I feel, in part, Your heavy load.
> Thank You for the desperate plea,
>   "God, why hast Thou forsaken Me?"
> "Because," You answer tenderly,
>   "I have a special plan for thee."
> Thank you for the hope You've given,
>   for the truth that You have risen.
> I, too, from suffering shall rise
>   as I fulfill Your plan so wise.
> Thank you, Lord, for letting me say,
>   "By grace I've suffered in Your way."
> And, may I nevermore depart
>   from this, the center of Your heart.
>   (Martha Baldock Fellure)

Pain will make us or break us. There is no middle ground. The landscape of life is littered with the pieces of fragile lives shattered by the blows of pain. Yet, by God's strength, there are those who stand among the broken pieces. They have taken the painful blows and transformed them by God's grace into opportunities for His glory. They are not made of stronger stuff, but they do have an understanding of the processes that preserve them in the midst of trouble. They have a working knowledge of the rules of the game. They have discovered what to do when it hurts.

3

The Terms of Engagement
Playing by the Rules

Ed Harrell, a former trustee of the Moody Bible Institute, served in World War II as a Marine. Near the close of the war he was assigned with just a few other Marines to a highly classified task. The assignment was so classified that they were not told its purpose or given more than a brief explanation of what they were to do. They were to proceed to San Francisco, where they would pick up a large crate that had been sent to San Francisco from Nevada. They were to guarantee that that crate was aboard the USS *Indianapolis* when it sailed from port and to stand watch over that cargo until it was dropped off at a small island in the Pacific. Obedient, but totally unaware of the purpose of the mission, the men delivered their assigned cargo to the Pacific island and remained aboard the *Indianapolis* as it set sail for the Philippines. So confidential was their mission that when the ship left the island for the Philippines its departure was unannounced and its ultimate port of arrival not made known to the men.

In transit from that island the USS *Indianapolis* was hit by three successive Japanese torpedoes. In a brief time the ship went down, leaving those who had survived the attack floating in life jackets in the ocean. No one in the outside world knew that they were there or that their ship had sunk.

For four and a half days Ed Harrell floated in his life jacket in the Pacific. He started in a group of eighty, who made a large circle arm and arm in the ocean, encouraging each other and hoping that someone would see them and rescue them. After two days that group of eighty had dwindled to seventeen. The rest had broken away from the group and been attacked by sharks, or they had died as a consequence of drinking salt water from the ocean, creating a chemical imbalance in their bodies that brought on disorientation, hallucinations, and eventually death, as they disappeared beneath the waves.

Miraculously, after four days the group—now numbering five—was noticed by a pilot flying at three thousand feet over the ocean. An oil slick on one of their now soggy, only partially supportive life jackets had reflected a flash of sunlight that caught the eye of the pilot, who was part of a sub-sweeping operation.

Three days after their departure from that tiny Pacific island the atom bomb was dropped on Hiroshima and Nagasaki, ending the war and saving an estimated hundreds of thousands of lives that would have been lost in a prolonged land war in the Japanese theater.

Parts to those bombs had been in the crate they had delivered.

I asked Ed how he could possibly have resisted drinking water from ocean all those days. His reply was simple. In his training as a Marine he had been drilled time and time again on the dangers of drinking salt water should he ever be marooned in the ocean. His training demanded that men stranded in the ocean should always stay together and never drink the water, regardless of how bad it got. Ed's commitment to stick to the rules no matter how critical the situation brought him through the crisis successfully.

> *Getting through trouble victoriously*
> *requires a willingness to know*
> *and play by the rules.*

Our success in the midst of suffering demands a response not unlike Ed's. God often assigns us to circumstances we don't understand or places us in situations about which we know little. Yet in the midst of those divinely classified encounters, He asks of us simply to trust Him and obey. When in the process we are torpedoed by unexpected crises, it is paramount that regardless of how we feel, or how deeply we are tempted to do otherwise, we respond according to the biblical principles, that will ultimately bring us through. As tough as it seems, stalwart submission to biblical patterns of response is the key to success.

Simply stated, getting through trouble victoriously requires a willingness to know and play by the rules. I can't expect to succeed at basketball simply by being placed on a court in tennis shoes and being handed a ball. Nor would it be enough to be told that the object of the game was for my team to place the ball through the hoop more often than our opponents. If that's all we knew about the game, we would soon be frustrated participants. The first time someone stole the ball from us or blocked a shot, we'd shout, "Unfair!" Yet that's all part of the game. We would feel cheated only because we didn't know the rules.

We would then be left with a choice. We could pout in the middle of the court, stomp off the floor, and tell everyone how much we dislike the referee and the game of basketball, or we could regroup, learn more about the game, get back in, and participate successfully.

Living is much like that. If we imagine that life consists simply of being born, being saved, being comfortable, dying, and going to heaven, then we have misunderstood life and will probably be consumed by it.

> *Nothing—absolutely nothing— passes into our lives that He has not first sovereignly authorized.*

Existence here on earth is a highly competitive experience. It is a field dotted with land mines, a road full of potholes. And, though none of us asked to be put in this game called life, we find ourselves in the midst of its fast-paced, confusing, often painful scramble. We can choose how to respond. We can adjust to the fundamental rules of the game, or we can fight against them. No one has ever won by bucking the rules, and plenty of good people have been benched by bitterness.

John Wooden, for many years the basketball coach of the UCLA Bruins, once stated that the key to his many national championships was his capacity to get his teams to master the fundamentals.

If pain is to make us and not break us, then we too must master the fundamentals.

Three fundamental principles form the foundation of successful responses to trouble. When we respond to pain in the context of those truths, it will be the beginning of more than survival. It will be the beginning of outright victory. Keeping those fundamentals in place will allow pain to become a productive agent of change in our lives and show a watching world the enormous power of God's grace and glory.

Affirming those fundamentals requires that we are willing to bypass the question, "Why?" Going no further than seeking an answer to the why of tragedy is a futile exercise that often leads only to greater despair. God does not always tell us the why. But because God —who is just, fair, loving, and full of grace and truth—is overseeing the trauma, we can live without knowing all of the whys. Making our way out of the thicket of question marks that so often crowd the crises of life can be accomplished when we cling to those three fundamentals that are true about God, who guarantees crisis by His permission, His nature, and His presence.

GOD'S SOVEREIGN PERMISSION

The first certainty to which we must cling is that *everything* that comes into our lives comes through *the sovereign permission* of God.

The Chicago Stadium is the home of the mighty Chicago Bulls. For several seasons, now, every home game has been sold out far in advance. There are only so many entrances to the stadium. At each entrance is a guard who keeps out anyone who does not have permission to enter. Only those who have been granted a ticket can get through. Everyone else is excluded.

God is like that. He is the gatekeeper of our lives. Some crises he permits to enter our lives, but others He turns away. Knowing our limits, He denies them entrance.

With God, nothing—absolutely *nothing*—passes into our lives that He has not first sovereignly authorized.

When Satan came to God in Job 1, he claimed that Job loved God only because God had abundantly blessed him. Satan charged God with having to buy Job's loyalty and favor: "Have you not put a hedge around him and his household and everything he has?" (Job 1:8). Satan used the blessings God gave Job as the basis for questioning God's worthiness to receive Job's unqualified allegiance regardless of blessing or buffeting. God listened while Satan slandered His glory before the watching hosts of the universe. Then He made a remarkable counter-proposal. Job was to have the privilege of demonstrating in the arena of human existence that God is utterly worthy of man's worship, praise, and allegiance, even when all of life falls apart.

God therefore gave Satan permission to test the depth of Job's allegiance. He permitted Satan to withdraw all the blessings of home and health, yet at the same time God blocked Satan from taking Job's life (Job 1:12). God stood as the sentinel at the gate of Job's existence.

Not only does the story of Job illustrate God's work in permitting or excluding pain, but God's very nature as a sovereign, all-knowing, all-powerful God guarantees this foundational principle. God is sovereignly and ultimately in control of all the universe (Job 38-41). His sovereign rule guarantees His oversight of the affairs of man (Numbers 23:19; Isaiah 37:16). His omniscience assures us that He is totally aware of all that transpires (Psalm 139:1-6). His power guarantees that He is able to withhold or permit all that seeks to intrude into our lives (2 Corinthians 13:4; Philippians 3:21).

Yet, though it is true that all trouble comes through the sovereign permission of God, it is also true from a human standpoint that there are different ways in which the trouble may come.

Some pain is caused *directly by Satan.* Job's experience is the classic example. Though trouble that is personally directed at us by the singular hand of Satan himself would not be the norm, it does remain a possibility.

Problems may come to us because of the *disobedience and carelessness of others.* The agony of Joseph's separation from his family was a direct result of the willful sin of his brothers.

There are times when pain enters the door of *our own disobedience or carelessness* (1 Peter 2:19-20). The prophet Jonah purposely disobeyed God's command to preach to Nineveh, and the trauma of a three-day assignment in a sleazy, underwater "hotel" became his portion.

At times our difficulties may be permitted by God as *a direct result of our obedience.* The disciples obediently took the boat across the lake, and even though they obeyed, they experienced a storm that threatened their lives. That storm was used by God to teach them a firsthand lesson in faith (Mark 4:35-41).

It is possible at times that traumatic situations in our lives may come from *a combination of these sources.* God's word indicates, for instance, that the crucifixion of Christ was a multiple involvement of God's direct action combined with the wicked actions of those who nailed Him to the cross. Acts 2:23 states, "This man was handed over to you by God's set purpose and foreknowledge; and you, with the help of wicked men, put him to death by nailing him to the cross."

Although it is helpful to understand the sources of trouble, it is vital to embrace the concept that, above it all and regardless of it all, what occurs takes place by God's permission. The principle of God's properly understood permission provides a source of encouragement and security in the midst of pain. How frightening it would be if our trials could escape the notice and permission of God. How helpless and vulnerable we would be.

One evening after soccer practice, I was walking home from high school when three men jumped my friend and me and began beating us for no apparent reason. I recall seeing a man walking toward us; I thought that he would surely come to our defense. As we called for help, he calmly walked by, ignoring our pleas for help. Our only glimmer of hope was gone. We were left at the mercy of those who mugged us. By contrast, no believer ever needs to feel the helpless agony of sensing that God is unaware and uninterested. We can have the settled security of knowing that nothing circumvents God's authority. God is aware of, and attentive to our plight.

The Swedish hymn by Lionel Sandelberg says it best:

> More secure is no one ever
> Than the loved ones of the Savior,
> Not yon star on high abiding
> Nor the bird in home nest hiding.
>
> God His own doth tend and nourish,
> In His holy courts they flourish;
> Like a father kind He spares them,
> In His loving arms He bears them.
>
> Neither life nor death can ever
> From the Lord His children sever,
> For His love and deep compassion
> Comforts them in tribulation.
>
> Little flock, joy then yield thee!
> Jacob's God will ever shield thee;
> Rest secure with this defender
> At His will also surrender.
>
> What He takes or what He gives us
> Shows the Father's love so precious;
> We may trust His purpose holy
> 'Tis His children's welfare solely.

So, understanding that all my pain is by God's permission is a foundational element of the rules of engagement. Yet in and of itself embracing this principle alone is not sufficient. Without the second certainty, we may be tempted to think that in permitting the crisis we are enduring, God is cruel, unfair, and without love or sensitivity.

GOD'S ETERNAL CONSISTENCY

The second fundamental is that God's permission is always *consistent with and guaranteed by His nature.* God cannot be unfaithful to Himself.

Skeptics often ask, "Can God make a rock so big that He cannot move it?" No matter how you answer the riddle, you limit God. If He cannot move the rocks that He makes, He is not all-powerful. If He cannot create rocks that big, His power to create is limited. The right answer to the question is that God cannot do anything contrary to His nature. Since He is true, He cannot lie. Since He is loving, He cannot do anything inconsistent with His love. Since He is just, He can never be unjust. Since He is perfect in every aspect of His existence, He cannot do anything to violate that perfection. He can only be and only do those things that are consistent with Himself. As Paul puts it, "He cannot disown himself" (2 Timothy 2:13).

> *God . . . actively involves Himself in meeting our needs. No trouble can separate us from this reality.*

God's intrinsic nature guarantees all that He does. He does what He does because of what He is.

Each morning I get up, shave, shower, and dress. I go to the office, study, manage, interact with staff and colleagues, leave my office for lunch, and then return to the office. About 2:00 P.M. I consider lying down for fifteen minutes, but the phone buzzes—and there is another call to take, another issue to deal with, another article to write, another letter to answer.

Dogs are quite different.

Our dog, Paddington, gets up when she wants, eats when she wants, goes outdoors when she wants, comes in when she wants. When she wants to sleep, she drops on the spot and sleeps as long as she wishes.

There are times when I wouldn't mind being a dog. But I can't. My humanity is intrinsic to me. I didn't choose to be human, I *am* human. My human nature dictates that who I am and what I do is consistent with the reality of my humanity.

So it is with God. He cannot be what He is not. This truth has relevance to the problem of pain and the certainty of His permission. Since God cannot violate His nature. His permissive decisions must be consistent with what He is. That guarantees that God is never destructive, malicious, or wrong in what He permits. We must always view the pain that has been permitted in the context of God's nature.

For starters, some of the qualities that are consistent with God bear particular relevance to the things that He permits within our lives.

One of those qualities is God's *goodness* (Psalm 34:8; Romans 8:28). It is difficult to see the goodness of God in the context of our pain. Yet the psalmist writes, "Taste and see that the Lord is good" (Psalm 34:8). Often we equate goodness with painlessness, comfort, and peace. That is an insufficient equation. Surgery is good. Birth is good. Even the truth that hurts is good. There are aspects of life we readily recognize as painful, yet good.

We must also distinguish between goodness and comfortableness. Comfort is not always good, and goodness is not always comfortable. God may not always be comfortable, but He is always good, and all that He permits can come to ultimate good both for our own sakes and for His glory (Romans 8:28-29).

All that God permits is guaranteed by His *creative power* (Genesis 50:20; Romans 5:3-5; James 1:2-5). God's power to take the most negative situations and turn them into positive realities worthy of His praise is demonstrated throughout biblical history. There is not a crisis that goes beyond the bounds of God's creative power. Whether the difficulties come from Satan or other people, or are self-inflicted, or are experienced in the process of our obedience, it is the prerogative of God to rearrange, reconstruct, reinterpret, and realign the situation to bring glory and praise to His name. When Joseph stood before his brothers, who had injured him deeply, he proclaimed, "You intended to harm me, but God intended it for good to accomplish what is now being done, the saving of many lives" (Genesis 50:20). Even Christ's death on the cross was transformed by the power of God into the positive results and residual benefits of the redemption that many of us have come to know and enjoy.

Since God is *just,* all that He permits is consistent with His justice. We may feel that God has cheated us or treated us unfairly because we have been dished out a portion of pain. But "the Lord loves justice, and does not forsake His godly ones. They are preserved forever" (Psalm 37:28, NASB).

God's justice guarantees that ultimately all that is unfair will be dealt with. We are naive to assume that all of life in its fallen condition will be fair and just. It is only safe to realize that God is just and that in His time and in His own way He will deal with both the injustice and those who have been unjust. Paul writes that God "will pay back trouble to those who trouble you and give relief to you who are troubled" (2 Thessalonians 1:6-7).

Since God is *holy* (Psalm 145:17), all He does is consistent with that holiness. To say that God is holy is to say that He is totally unlike all others in His perfection. He *cannot* make a mistake. God's holiness is a foundational attribute of His nature. It is also a foundational support for us in the midst of our pain. The behavior of our holy God is impeccable, flawless. He is "holy in all His works" (Psalm 145:17, KJV*), even in those works that cause us trauma.

God's *total awareness,* better known as His omniscience (1 Corinthians 10:13; 2 Peter 2:9), is also relevant to our experience of pain. It is significant that God knows all about us, because He has promised that He will permit no trial to come into our lives that is beyond what we can bear (1 Corinthians 10:13). Since He knows our "load limit," He limits our load.

God's total awareness lifts our sense of despair. In difficulty, our despair is deepened when we sense that there is no way out. Trouble can be like a room with no doors and no windows, a room with walls that are closing in. I love the verse that says, "The Lord knows how to rescue godly men from trials" (2 Peter 2:9). When there seems to be no possibility of release, God already knows how to deliver us. In fact, He has options we have never dreamed of.

God's *perfect timing* is also relevant to our struggle (Psalm 31:14-15). God is always on time—never too early, never too late. Shadrach, Meshach, and Abednego probably wondered if God's sense of timing was a touch off as the guards pushed them into the fire. But it was in the fire that God met them and gave them a testimony to turn a pagan king's heart to the true and living God (Daniel 3:4-30). As the psalmist affirms, "I trust in you,

*King James Version.

O Lord; I say, 'You are my God.' My times are in your hands" (Psalm 31:14-15a).

God's *certain purpose* is another source of comfort (Romans 8:28-29). God never wastes our sorrows. In Him, there is purpose in pain. There is the purpose of character development (conforming to His image), the purpose of becoming useful in His service, the purpose of purifying our lives and values, the purpose of gaining a new sense of God's sufficiency, becoming more effective in ministry, and developing a closer identity with Christ.

Our God is a God of purpose. He grants pain only with a productive end in mind. That is why it is said of Christ that He willingly endured the cross for "the joy set before him" (Hebrews 12:2).

God's *unfailing love* (Romans 8:35-39) is an indispensable part of His nature in the time of trouble. It is because God consistently loves us that Paul could ask:

> Who shall separate us from the love of Christ? Shall trouble or hardship or persecution or famine or nakedness or danger or sword? . . . No, in all these things we are more than conquerors through him who loved us. For I am convinced that neither death nor life, neither angels nor demons, neither the present nor the future, nor any powers, neither height nor depth, nor anything else in all creation, will be able to separate us from the love of God that is in Christ Jesus our Lord. (Romans 8:35, 37-39)

God loves us and actively involves Himself in meeting our needs. No trouble can separate us from this reality.

The more we know what God is like, the more confidence we gain in terms of His role as the guardian at the gate of our lives.

GOD'S CONTINUAL PRESENCE WITH US

The third fundamental truth to which we must cling is the reality of *God's continual presence with us.* God's promise that He will never leave us nor forsake us enables us to say with confidence, "The Lord is my helper, I will not be afraid. What shall man do to me?" (Hebrews 13:6). The presence of God is not unlike His assurance to Israel through the prophet Isaiah:

> Fear not: for I have redeemed thee, I have called thee by thy name; thou art mine. When thou passest through the waters, I will be with thee; and through the rivers, they shall not overflow thee: when thou walkest through the fire, thou shalt not be burned; neither shall the flame kindle upon thee. For I am the Lord thy God, the Holy One of Israel, thy Saviour. (Isaiah 43:1-3, KJV)

God assured Joshua, "Have I not commanded you? Be strong and courageous. Do not be terrified; do not be discouraged, for the Lord your God will be with you wherever you go" (Joshua 1:9).

The struggle we have with this truth no doubt is that though we are willing to admit that He is with us, we often have difficulty sensing His presence. An old story speaks to the issue. A weary pilgrim who had experienced many difficulties in life finally went home to be with the Lord. The Lord took him to the edge of heaven and showed him a long stretch of beach. "This beach is your life and that other set of footprints is Mine, walking beside you all the way." The pilgrim noted a portion of the beach where one set of footprints disappeared, and he said to God, "Why did You abandon me there? That was such a terrible time for me!" God replied, "I didn't abandon you. That is where I picked you up and carried you."

In his book *Angels: God's Secret Agents,* Billy Graham cites the story of John G. Paton, pioneer missionary in the New Hebrides Islands:

> Hostile natives surrounded his mission headquarters one night, intent on burning the Patons out and killing them. John Paton and his wife prayed all during that terror-filled night that God would deliver them. When daylight came they were amazed to see that, unaccountably, the attackers had left. They thanked God for delivering them.
> A year later, the chief of the tribe was converted to Jesus Christ, and Mr. Paton, remembering what had happened, asked the chief what had kept him and his men from burning down the house and killing them. The chief replied in surprise, "Who were all those men you had with you there?" The missionary answered, "There were no men there, just my wife and I." The chief argued that they had seen many men standing guard—hundreds of big men in shining garments with drawn swords in their hands. They seemed to circle the mission station so that the natives were afraid to attack. Only then did Mr. Paton realize that God had sent His angels to protect them. The chief agreed that there was no other explanation.[1]

Paton's story brings to mind the psalmist's assertion "The angel of the Lord encamps around those who fear Him, and rescues them" (Psalm 34:7, NASB).

We may be unaware of the Lord's presence or of the power His presence brings to our trauma. But He *is* there, walking with us, helping us, and leading us with grace to glory!

1. Billy Graham, *Angels: God's Secret Agents* (New York: Doubleday, 1975), pp. 16-17.

A Source of Refuge and Strength

Even amidst the cruelties of war, rules govern many aspects of the conflict. Some of those rules have to do with prisoners of war; others have to do with the way the conflict is engaged. Some have to do with the weapons that are permitted; others have to do with procedures agreed upon by the enemies.

So it is with us in the midst of suffering.

There are principles that cannot and must not be compromised. They govern the engagement. Those who trust those rules of conflict will find great security and refuge, even in life's darkest hours. The reality of *God's permission* for all that enters our lives, *guaranteed* by that which is *consistent* with His nature and undergirded by His *unfailing presence* are certain rules of engagement. Grasping these nonnegotiable principles is essential to our successful response to trouble. They lead us to find *refuge and strength* in God. Is it any wonder that God's Word commands us to be "strong *in the Lord*" (Ephesians 6:10, italics added)?

We can choose . . . the question marks of uncertainty . . . or . . . the exclamation points of that which is certain.

One of Satan's first strategic assaults on our stability in the midst of suffering will be to attack our confidence in God. You can count on it. If he can somehow get us to blame God and turn our backs on Him, he has won the day and our undoing is sure. If you have ever walked through a swamp, you know that your feet are constantly searching for something solid to stand on—a rock, a stump, or dry ground. When we find something solid, we put our weight on it for stability. Though we are still in the swamp, we are safe and secure.

We can choose to sink in the mire of the question marks of uncertainty, or we can cling to the exclamation points of that which is certain.

In the midst of Job's suffering, his wife counseled him to "curse God and die!" (Job 2:9) But Job refused to do so. He affirmed, "Though he slay me, yet will I trust in him" (Job 13:15, KJV). Since Job knew that God could not deny Himself and the solid foundation of His nature, Job would not deny his God.

Where is God when it hurts? He is right there at the gate of our existence, guaranteeing all that comes by His changeless nature and granting to us the assurance of His loving presence.

> Hast thou not known? hast thou not heard, that the everlasting God, the Lord, the Creator of the ends of the earth, fainteth not, neither is weary? there is no searching of His understanding. He giveth power to the faint; and to them who have no might he increaseth strength. Even the youths shall faint and be weary, and the young men shall utterly fall: but they that wait upon the Lord shall renew their strength; they shall mount up with wings as eagles; they shall run, and not be weary; and they shall walk, and not faint. (Isaiah 40:28-31, KJV)

In times of trouble we must resist the question marks of "Why?" and concentrate on "Who?" Once we understand who it is that stands beside us in trouble, our confidence will be strong. When we trust in Him, He will teach us how to triumph in our pain and and reach the point of glory.

4

What Is Going On?
Understanding the Trouble
That Troubles Us

God rarely fills out the "Why?" section of the questionnaire we send to Him when trouble enters our lives. Beyond the general truth that pain is a process with the purpose of growth and glory, specific personalized reasons for the struggle we endure are rarely given this side of eternity. God tells us that in a coming day He will wipe away every tear from our eyes and that there shall no longer be any crying (Revelation 21:4). I often wonder if it isn't then that He will explain it all, and, finally knowing the why, we will find that our tears have turned to joy, our lips to praise.

The challenge in the here and now is to get beyond the "whys" by focusing on the right question, "Who?" The answer is found in seeing Him clearly as we learn to cling to the certainty of His guardianship over our lives that is guaranteed by His character and the abiding reality of His presence. Affirming that He gives grace and works all things to our growth and the good of His glory liberates us to look in His direction and, instead of blaming Him, yield to Him and His purposes.

Trials Reveal What We Are Really Like

As we walk in this discipline of trust, our hope is then free to focus on the questions, "What is going on in this difficulty?" "What is God doing?" "What is He doing to me?" Scripture clearly answers those questions.

James 1:2 uses a specific word for trouble that leads to a helpful understanding of what trouble is. The essence of this word led J. B. Phillips to paraphrase the passage by saying that when troubles come, "don't resent them as intruders, but welcome them as friends!"*

When James says, "Consider it all joy, my brethren, when you encounter various trials" (James 1:2, NASB), his choice of words is strategic. The Greek word for "trial" is a word that means to examine or test for the purpose of proving or revealing something about the thing tested. It is a test that reveals something for a specific purpose. Of all the things we could say about trials —that they are disappointing, discouraging, humiliating, uncomfortable, painful, and disheartening—God, among other reasons, sees them as tests that reveal our true selves. It's a sure thing that in trouble, the real me becomes apparent quickly. Trouble is revelatory.

Trouble is one of God's ways of examining our lives. When we are on easy street—and thank the Lord that He lets us come up for air periodically—it is hard for us to know what we are really like. We can carry on a cosmetic existence and fool ourselves, and most of the people, about our true nature.

But when trouble hits our lives, what we are really like is quickly revealed. Trouble shows our friends, our spouses, our children, and our acquaintances what we

*J. B. Phillips, *The New Testament in Modern English*, rev. ed. (New York: Macmillan, 1947, 1957).

are like. Even more unsettling, it forces us to start seeing ourselves for what we really are.

I am committed to the sanctification process in my
life, to becoming increasingly pure as I grow in my walk
with God. Yet sanctification is tough, even in situations
that are not life-threatening. When my son is playing
basketball, it's a trial to see him sitting on the bench
when he ought to be playing. A small trial, but a revealing one. Worse yet is what it's like when he gets into the
game and the referee starts to harass him. Rising out of
my seat, I begin to "express myself," only to feel my
wife tug at my coat: "Joe, you're the president of Moody
Bible Institute!" There is much in me that needs to be
worked on. More important than the "obvious lack of
judgment by the coach or the referee" is my lack of maturity in terms of self-control and Christlikeness. The
pressure of the "trial" during the game gives me a good
look at myself and shows me areas in which I need to
grow.

Without that strategic perspective, we tend to focus on the external aspects of our problems. Yet if we
keep in mind that trouble is in part intended to reveal
the real "me" so that we may grow, our focus in pain
will move from "pity" to "production" in terms of God's
glory in and through us.

---

*Trouble . . . reveals where I am in
. . . terms of my conformity to the
image and character of Christ.*

Have you ever been listening to the radio when the
normal programming is interrupted for a test of the National Defense System? The ordinary schedule is set
aside to test the readiness of the station to meet an
emergency. That's exactly what God's tests do in our

lives. God interrupts the normal programming to say, "This is a test. Let's take a look at where you are."

Because I live thirty miles west of Chicago I leave home early in the morning to beat the traffic. One of the things I love to do on that drive is to worship God, with the help of cassette tapes and the radio. I'll never forget the morning I was listening to the Brooklyn Tabernacle Choir. One hundred and eighty voices, saved off the streets of Brooklyn, singing like they meant it, with energy and power, were lifting me before the Lord as I sang and worshiped. As I approached the city, the sun was rising behind the cityscape. Through the morning haze, rays of beautiful orange cast their shafts between the buildings. My heart thought, *What a glorious Creator we have.* I was in ecstasy!

Pulling up to a stoplight, I noticed a taxicab facing me with his left blinker on and his wheel cranked to the left. He kept inching forward. I knew what he had in his heart. *He wants to cut me off when the light turns green!* And so, right in the midst of my worship, God said, "We interrupt the normal programming for this test." Because I was in such close fellowship with God at that moment you would think that I would let the taxicab by, since it's important to be understanding and loving. After all, maybe the taxi driver was late for breakfast and his wife was waiting for him. Maybe he had just got a call from a woman in labor. Whatever— here was my opportunity to reveal the true nature of my worship.

The light turned green, and I nailed the accelerator. The taxi driver nailed his, too, and he just missed me as I went flying by. He was making a U-turn, and we ended up at the next light next to each other. You know, we Christians have such a limited set of gestures to use. All I could do was to look at him, throw my hands up and say, "What are you doing?" The light turned green, and I drove on. But when I walked through those legacy-laden arches at Moody, the Spirit said, "Stowell, we got a good look at you this morning. There's something to work on in your life!"

What good is trouble? Among other things, it reveals where I am in the growth process in terms of my conformity to the image and character of Christ. It gets me beyond assumptions to reality. Am I a forgiving person? Am I kind? Understanding? Just? Loving? Helpful? Patient? Or am I angry, slanderous, self-centered, inflexible, manipulative, weak, and ill-equipped to respond to trials correctly?

It is helpful to see ourselves as we really are. Trouble reveals that, and it turns the agenda toward the things in *our* lives that need to be changed, so that we can grow to be more like Him—and that, of course, is the purpose of our redemption (Romans 8:28-29) and one of God's purposes in trials (James 1:2-4).

William Coltman was pastor of Highland Park Baptist Church in Detroit, Michigan, for more than forty years. He served with dignity through many difficult times. At one point in his life he was falsely accused of moral indiscretion, and his wife, who was not completely balanced mentally, refused to go to church with him. Each Sunday she left the house to attend another church down the street.

His secretary of many years told me that through it all she "never heard him say a negative word about anyone!" In the test, his character was revealed, and Christ was glorified.

What are trials anyway? Often they are tests to let us know where we are in the process of growing up in Him.

James 1:2 goes on to qualify the nature of these tests by saying that "many kinds" of trials will enter our lives. Knowing what kind of trouble to expect is a great help in being ready to meet that trouble.

The Scripture speaks of at least seven different kinds of trouble.

TRIALS OF PLACE AND RACE

First, and probably most common, are trials of *place* and *race*. Scripture affirms that we live in a fallen place. This planet is under the rule of our adversary, Satan. Earth is his domain. We are also part of a fallen race. Apart from the help of God, all of us are prone to express our fallenness in all kinds of damaging ways.

We can count on it, living in a fallen place and being a part of a fallen race is going to produce difficult times. Originally, this place was a perfect environment where productive work, fellowship with God, and morally responsible actions provided fulfillment and unhindered joy. But in Genesis 3, sin entered the picture and raped the scene. The rest of Scripture speaks to the struggle of real people trying to live in a fallen place as part of a fallen race.

The wonderful thing about the scope of biblical history is that whereas it starts with a perfect creation and then records the Fall, it ends with the glorious consummation of all things. One of my all-time favorite passages in Scripture is in Revelation: "The former things are passed away. . . . Behold I make all things new" (Revelation 21:4b-5a, KJV). What a great hope for us. In that new environment there will be no more death, no more tears, no more sorrow, no more pain, no more crying. But until then, we are a *fallen race* planted in a *fallen place.*

When we were children we played the game "So Big." We couldn't wait to grow up. Then we became teenagers. We looked in the mirror and said, "No way! That can't be my body!" Our faces erupted like volcanoes, we started to become men and women, and we didn't like what was happening to us. Then we reached the thirties and our bodies began to slow down. We spent vast sums of money at health spas. Our bodies sagged and wrinkled, and we started looking for the plastic surgeon.

We look forward to retirement, but our bodies will retire before we do. Our back goes out more often than we do. When we lean down to pick something up, we want to stay down to see how many other things we can get now that we're there.

Our bodies get sick. And rarely on schedule. Some of us carry bodies that are diseased. Arthritis, diabetes, and Alzheimer's disease plague many. An upstanding person can contract AIDS from a transfusion at the hospital. The grim reaper stands ready to rob us of those we love in untimely and unsettling ways. It's a fallen place and we're a fallen race. Trouble comes with the territory.

From our bodies to fallen people who use, manipulate, and abuse us, to accidents, to killer tornadoes and devastating earthquakes, it's all part of being planted on a planet damaged by the rule of Satan and sin.

> *Now more than ever we ... must be prepared to pass the test of trials that come because of our identification with Christ.*

When a trial of place and race impacts our lives, what ought to be revealed? In 2 Corinthians 12, Paul valiantly struggles with his thorn in the flesh. He prays three times that God will remove it from him. But it is clear that it is not God's will that the thorn should be removed. It has purpose. So Paul acknowledges the thorn's presence and recognizes that it has purpose, and he submits to the trial without bitterness or blaming God and claims that in his weakness God will become strong through his life.

Ernie Harwell has been the radio voice of the Detroit Tigers for decades. One of the few announcers to be appointed to the Baseball Hall of Fame, Ernie has become synonymous with Detroit baseball. Ernie is a true legend in his own time. Few people know more about baseball facts and figures and are able to add more color and interest to the commentary of the game than Ernie Harwell.

Yet at the age of seventy-two, Ernie received the news from the new senior management of the Tigers and radio station WJR that when the next season was completed, his contract would not be fulfilled. It was one of those sudden and startling things that happens often in the sports world to coaches and players and, periodically, to broadcasters. To the masses of people who knew and loved Ernie, and to avid Tiger fans across the nation, this was cruel and unjust treatment of a man who still had much to give and who was closely linked to the Tiger legacy. What a man like Ernie Harwell deserved was time to wind down on his own and then a great celebration for the contribution he had made. Instead, after the '91 season, he would be "on the street."

Detroit went into a rage. All the major newspapers carried headlines denouncing the decision, and bumper stickers sprouted up everywhere pledging allegiance to Ernie and cleverly denouncing those who had forced his exit from baseball.

Concurrently, Lulu, his wife, discovered that she had cancer. It was a devastating double blow. But for Ernie and Lulu it all was the natural consequence of living in a fallen place and being part of a fallen race. Bad stuff just happens. It didn't seem fair or right or just, but the world is not a fair or just place.

Ernie Harwell is a committed believer in Jesus Christ. Throughout his years with the Tigers, his integrity had not gone unnoticed. One headline stretched across the top of a major Detroit paper read, "Gentleman Wronged."

As I read the press clippings my friends in Detroit sent me, I could see the real Ernie being revealed in the midst of a trial of place and race. A reporter asked him, "Are you bitter?" Ernie replied, "Bitter? Not a chance. The Lord's been too good to this tongue-tied boy from Georgia for too long for me to be bitter."

TRIALS OF TEMPTATION

The second kind of trial we find in Scripture is the trial of temptation. In Matthew 4:1 we read, "Then Jesus was led by the Spirit into the desert to be tempted by the devil." Interestingly enough, the same Greek word sometimes translated by the word "trial" is translated here by the word "tempted." Satan led Christ through the temptation of the pride of life and the lust of the flesh. He hit Christ at every vulnerable point we struggle with as humans. Temptation is an unavoidable part of our lives. It intrudes into the life of the businessman on the road, the homemaker in her house, the citizen filling out income tax forms, and the person who has been hurt by others. We feel the temptation to strike out in revenge, to gossip, or to slander. These are significant trials. Temptation puts life in stress. It's trouble.

In Matthew 4, Christ countered His trouble at every point by a response from God's Word that kept Him unflinchingly loyal to God. I have a friend in the ministry who, after checking into his hotel, got on the elevator with two attractive young ladies. As the door closed, one of them said, "Hey, how about a little fun with us tonight?" Who would know? I love his response. He said, "It was like God pulled a curtain down in front of me, and on the curtain was Galatians 6:7, 'He that sows to the flesh shall reap the corruption of the flesh.'" In his heart he said no to them and yes to God. His relationship to God was more important than the seductive pleasure of sin.

When I was a little boy, someone wrote in my Bible, "This book will keep you from sin or sin will keep you from this book." In the face of troubling temptation, the power of God's Word is an indispensable ally. As the psalmist said, "Thy word have I hid in mine heart, that I might not sin against thee" (Psalm 119:11, KJV).

TRIALS OF IDENTIFICATION

A third kind of trial that we might expect is the test of identification. In chapters 15 and 17 of the gospel of John, Christ told His disciples that they could expect the world to be rough on them, as it had been on Him. They could expect to be thrown out of the synagogue, to be disowned by their families, and in some cases even to be murdered. All because they bore His name and were identified with His cause.

History records that because the early church broke bread at Communion and said, "This is the body of Christ," the culture of that day accused them of cannibalism. Christians claimed Communion as their love feast, and the culture of that day accused them of improprieties in those private observances. In the midst of this pressure, Peter encouraged the believers to persevere. He wrote a suffering church, "Live such good lives among the pagans that, though they accuse you of doing wrong, they may see your good deeds and glorify God on the day he visits us" (1 Peter 2:12).

And, he added,

> How is it to your credit if you receive a beating for doing wrong and endure it? But if you suffer for doing good

and you endure it, this is commendable before God. To this you were called, because Christ suffered for you, leaving you an example that you should follow in his steps.

"He committed no sin,
and no deceit was found in his mouth."

When they hurled their insults at him, he did not retaliate; when he suffered, he made no threats. Instead, he entrusted himself to him who judges justly. He himself bore our sins in his body on the tree, so that we might die to sins and live for righteousness; by his wounds you have been healed. (1 Peter 2:20-24)

Now that America is becoming more and more secularized, we can expect more trouble in an environment increasingly hostile toward the values of righteousness we hold dear. Now more than ever we as God's people must be prepared to pass the test of trials that come because of our identification with Christ.

---

*Not one trouble that God brings
into our lives as believers
. . . is punishment.*

I have a colleague at Moody who, prior to his coming to serve as senior vice president of media, was on the fast track upward with Cox newspapers, headquartered in Atlanta, Georgia. He had been the publisher of the *Springfield News* in Springfield, Ohio, and had served Cox as the publisher of the *Dayton Daily News* in Dayton, Ohio. In both settings, he had made the newspapers he managed profitable and was well thought of within the newspaper community.

As a Christian, Dennis applied biblical standards of righteousness to the decisions he made in the marketplace. Some of those decisions concerned advertisements. It is common for newspapers to reserve the right to advertise things they believe are constructive in the community and to withhold advertising for those things they believe are not helpful to their business or to the community at large. In light of that practice, Dennis eliminated advertisements for X-rated movies in the Dayton papers. He also refused to run notices and advertisements for gay and lesbian groups in the community.

Needless to say, that decision brought forth an outcry from the groups whose advertisements had been rejected. Yet Dennis remained committed to that which was righteous and true. The issue went to those in authority over him in Atlanta. Though they had backed him in similar decisions in the past, to his surprise they said he had to run the ads from the gay and lesbian groups or lose his job.

For Dennis, this was a trial of identification. He chose rather to identify with Christ than to continue in his career.

Hebrews 11:24-27 says of Moses:

> By faith Moses, when he had grown up, refused to be known as the son of Pharaoh's daughter. He chose to be mistreated along with the people of God rather than to enjoy the pleasures of sin for a short time. He regarded disgrace for the sake of Christ as of greater value than the treasures of Egypt, because he was looking ahead to his reward. By faith he left Egypt, not fearing the king's anger; he persevered because he saw him who is invisible.

To stand for Christ and His values in a hostile environment is bound to bring trials into our lives. As Christians, we must realize that throughout church history, most often the church has been planted in a hostile environment. In fact, rarely has the church thrived in a friendly context. More and more, there will be tests involving our identity with Jesus Christ.

In the midst of trials of identification, the pattern of success is to persist in righteousness, regardless. Peter wrote:

> Dear friends, do not be surprised at the painful trial you are suffering, as though something strange were happening to you. But rejoice that you participate in the sufferings of Christ, so that you may be overjoyed when his glory is revealed. If you are insulted because of the name of Christ, you are blessed, for the Spirit of glory and of God rests on you. If you suffer, it should not be as a murderer or thief or any other kind of criminal, or even as a meddler. However, if you suffer as a Christian, do not be ashamed, but praise God that you bear that name. (1 Peter 4:12-16)

Faithful perseverance is the strength to be demonstrated in a test of identification.

TRIALS OF DISCIPLINE

There are also trials of discipline. We need some clarification here. As noted earlier, not all difficulty is God's discipline. When difficulty impacts us, we are prone to think that God is chastising us. That may not be true. Not all difficulty is discipline. It may be a trial of place and race, or a trial of temptation, or a test of identification. But if it is discipline, it will be difficult. In discipline, God seeks to nudge our lives back to paths of righteousness.

Note the difference between punishment and discipline. Punishment is justice. Discipline is corrective. There is a vast difference between the two. There is not one trouble that God brings into our lives as believers that is punishment. Sin was punished on the cross. We are not in double jeopardy. Every sin that I have committed, or will commit, or am committing has been punished. Justice was meted out at the cross. But the corrective discipline of God comes along with sovereign nudges that inflict just enough pressure to alert me to the problem and to get me back on the track of righteousness.

Proverbs 3:11-12 states, "My son, do not despise the Lord's discipline and do not resent his rebuke, because the Lord disciplines those he loves, as a father the son he delights in." Hebrews 12 says that if you feel God disciplining you, rejoice. It's a sign of sonship. If He doesn't discipline you, you are not His child. I understand that kind of talk. I don't know how many times I've been places where I have wanted to put a little corrective pressure on someone else's child. But I had no right. The child was not my son or daughter. But with regard to my own children, not only do I have the right to "encourage" them into right paths when they get derailed, I have the responsibility, the stewardship as a parent, to do just that.

How are we to respond to trials of discipline? By not resisting them. They come from a loving father, and we need to open our hearts to these trials so that the Lord might correct us through them and put us on the right path.

There are many illustrations of this kind of trial in Scripture, but I cannot resist going to the Old Testament prophet Jonah. The word of God came to the prophet: "Jonah, I want you to go to Nineveh." He immediately said, "No!"

What would God do? He needed somebody to go to Nineveh, but the prophet had just said he was not going—and in fact was on his way somewhere else. Discipline was God's response. Sovereignly nudging Jonah back toward obedience. Back toward Nineveh.

Jonah was down in the hold of the ship, sound asleep.

Some of us say to ourselves, *If I sin I won't feel any peace. And I feel peace so it must be all right.* Yet many times we have so rationalized our way into sin, that we feel quite peaceful about it. Jonah's nap demonstrates that emotional peace is not a barometer of righteousness.

Jonah was so much at peace that he slept all the way through a storm. God had sent that storm to wake him up and bring him to his senses. But he kept sleeping. So God sent the captain of the ship down to see him. Sovereign nudge number two. The pagan ship captain shook Jonah and said, "Wake up! And pray to your God!" So Jonah got up and went to the deck of the ship. There the sailors were trying to find out who was responsible for their trouble.

They cast lots and gave everybody a number, including Jonah. As that ship tossed and turned under the delicate, sovereign hand of God, the lots were cast on the windswept deck—and wouldn't you know it, the lots pointed to Jonah. "Tell us," the sailors cried, "who is responsible for making all this trouble for us? What do you do? Where do you come from? What is your country? From what people are you?" (Jonah 1:8)

He had to give a testimony. "He answered, 'I am a Hebrew and I worship the Lord, the God of heaven, who made the sea and the land'" (v. 9).

You'd think that by this time Jonah ought to be dropping to his knees. Right? No. The trouble increased. "So they asked him, 'What should we do to you to make the sea calm down for us?'" (v. 11)

Jonah could have said, "I'll pray and repent and your problem will be over." But Jonah replied, "Pick me up and throw me into the sea . . . and it will become calm. I know that it is my fault that this great storm has come upon you" (v. 12). Jonah was saying, "I would rather die than obey God." Finally, in desperation, the sailors chucked him overboard. Now Jonah had won. God had nudged him and nudged him, and yet he had stubbornly maintained his sinful choice.

But when it comes to discipline, God has options we've never dreamed of. Just when Jonah thought he had won, God said to a great fish, "Do you see that boat? I want you to swim next to it, and when you see a splash, that's lunch." Jonah lived three days and three nights in that underwater hotel. He wrestled with God and refused to say "Uncle," until finally, after three days of devastating discipline, he said, "God, You win."

We can expect that when we sin, God will love us enough to keep working to bring us back to the course of righteousness. "The Lord disciplines those he loves" (Hebrews 12:6). And although this discipline is sometimes tough and troublesome, He does it because He loves us enough to keep us on safe and successful paths.

Passing the test of discipline demands cooperation with God. When I was a boy, we used to like to wrestle to see whose young male ego could be affirmed. As little kids, we'd get a guy down, sit on top of him, and put him in a full-Nelson until he said one liberating word.

"Uncle!"

And that's how we respond to God. A trial of discipline is intended to get our stubborn wills to say, "All right! Uncle! I'm yours. I repent and will gladly walk in righteousness."

TRIALS OF CONSEQUENCE FOR SIN

There are also trials that are the consequence for sin. Chuck Swindoll says it so well when he says, "We teach our children 1 John 1:9, 'If we confess our sins, He is faithful and just to forgive us our sins and to cleanse us from all unrighteousness,' which may tempt them to coast on grace." He goes on to say that "if we teach them 1 John 1:9, we must also teach them Galatians 6:8, 'For the one who sows to his own flesh shall from the flesh reap corruption.'"

Some of our trouble is a direct consequence of willful sin in our lives. Sin always brings consequences. Nobody is exempt. No one is clever enough, no one is subtle enough, no one is intelligent enough to sin and not bear its consequences. "Be self-controlled and alert. Your enemy the devil prowls around like a roaring lion looking for someone to devour" (1 Peter 5:8). In the Old Testament we read, "There is a way that seems right to a man, but in the end it leads to death" (Proverbs 14:12). Sin always brings despair and trouble. Even long after we are forgiven, the consequences may remain. Some will not be removed until that final glorious day of redemption.

Paul, having murdered Christians, couldn't shake the memories. In the first chapter of 1 Timothy he calls himself the worst of sinners. Yet, he used that consequence as a springboard to worship and praise.

> Even though I was once a blasphemer and a persecutor and a violent man, I was shown mercy because I acted in ignorance and unbelief. The grace of our Lord was poured out on me abundantly, along with the faith and love that are in Christ Jesus.
>
> Here is a trustworthy saying that deserves full acceptance: Christ Jesus came into the world to save sinners—of whom I am the worst. But for that very reason I was shown mercy so that in me, the worst of sinners, Christ Jesus might display his unlimited patience as an example for those who would believe on him and receive eternal life. Now to the King eternal, immortal, invisible, the only God, be honor and glory for ever and ever. Amen. (1 Timothy 1:13-17)

Living with the troubling and sometimes lifelong consequences of sin, we ought to be motivated by the reminder of the awfulness of our sin to say, "God, this living daily reminder reminds me of Your amazing grace to love, forgive, forget and receive me." It ought to be, as well, a protective shield to help us not to risk the path of sin again. And, significantly, it ought to make us take our hearts off this fleeting, fallen world and live for that grand and glorious day of redemption when all things are passed away, and, behold, all things will become new.

Trials of display give us the opportunity to prove . . . that God is still number one in our lives.

First John 3:2 proclaims, "Dear friends, now we are children of God, and what we will be has not yet been made known. But we know that when he appears, we shall be like him, for we shall see him as he is." I love this verse. Take heart. The consequence soon will pass. When He comes and we meet Him face to face, it will all be new. Consequences, even in our tears and brokenness, can be to praise and glory with a deepening love for God and His appearing instead of a heart soured and angry at God.

TRIALS OF DISPLAY

The sixth kind of trouble we might face is the trial of display. This kind of trial God permits to come to our lives to enable us to display something for Him through our trauma.

God came to Abraham and said, "Take your son, your only son, Isaac, whom you love, and go to the region of Moriah. Sacrifice him there as a burnt offering on one of the mountains I will tell you about" (Genesis 22:2).

Quite frankly, when I hear that God has required a child sacrifice, it troubles my spirit. I don't like to think that my God is like that. We have to note the context. In this particular context, Abraham is living in the land of the Canaanites, where the highest form of commitment to their gods of wood and stone was the taking of their children and sacrificing them to their pagan gods. The blood of their children was the pinnacle statement of commitment to their god.

I believe that God was saying to Abraham, "Are you willing to display your love for Me, the true and the living God, as much as these pagans are?" I think there was something even more significant in this trial, this test in Abraham's life. You see, Isaac was the gift God had given to Abraham. He was the miracle baby. Isaac was the whole reason Abraham left Ur of the Chaldees to become a pilgrim in the land of the Canaanites. Genesis 12:1-2, the passage that gives God's command to Abraham to leave Ur, is the first prophetic statement of the coming of Christ: "The Lord had said to Abram, 'Leave your country, your people and your father's household and go to the land I will show you. I will make you into a great nation and I will bless you; I will make your name great, and you will be a blessing.'"

Years went by, and Abraham and Sarah were past childbearing age. Then, suddenly, miraculously, God gave them the gift of this boy. Abraham loved Isaac. I believe God was asking Abraham, "Do you love the gift more than the giver?"

God often marches into our lives and threatens something precious to us. Something He has given us. A child, a house, a spouse, a career. How do we respond? Do we display through our response that we love the giver more than the gift? That He is still first in the league of our living?

I root for the Detroit Tigers and, regardless, remain a loyal fan. During baseball season, every morning I open up the newspaper to see where the Tigers stand in the American League East. God opens the newspaper of our lives to see whether He is still first —or what has displaced Him. Only you can answer that question. You may be asked to give that answer through a trial of display.

Abraham wakes up his boy on that morning and they walk for three days. Abraham has a long time to change his mind, to flunk the test. He has three whole days of walking to say, "God, you're not first. Isaac is first in my life." And he walks three days, builds the altar, lays down his son—and now the marvelous statement of what kind of God our God is. God says, "Wait! That's all! That's all!" Genesis 22:12 puts it this way: "Do not lay a hand on the boy. . . . Do not do anything to him. Now I know that you fear God, because you have not withheld from me your son, your only son."

Trials of display give us the opportunity to prove to God, to ourselves, and to a watching world that God is still number one in our lives.

Some trials of display are intended to be a platform where God's power can be clearly seen. Such is the case with the man born blind (John 9:1-3).

> As he went along, [Jesus] saw a man blind from birth. His disciples asked him, "Rabbi, who sinned, this man or his parents, that he was born blind?"
>
> "Neither this man nor his parents sinned," said Jesus, "but this happened so that the work of God might be displayed in his life."

The blind man's trouble had nothing to do with the consequence of sin. His blindness was, instead, a platform upon which the glory and power of God could be seen. I often wonder what works of God are displayed in the midst of my trouble? Forgiveness, kindness, patience, grace? Or is my trouble a platform for Satan's agenda?

TRIALS OF BROKEN EXPECTATIONS

The last kind of trial is the trial of broken expectations. You and I need to remember that one of the greatest difficulties we have in life is dealing with expectations that never come to pass. In fact, most counselors will tell you that much depression comes from the disappointment that comes from broken expectations.

When we get married we have expectations. Newly married husbands expect a lot of things from their wives. And she has a whole list of expectations for him. He is expecting her to pick up after him, prepare wonderful meals, care for the brood, exhibit social graces, work like a "strong bull at home," have the kids corralled, set a beautiful table with sterling candlesticks, have his favorite meal ready for him when he comes home, and after the meal—while he reads the paper—finish the work in the kitchen, put the kids to bed, and then be a tiger in the bedroom.

She has her list as well. He will be sensitive, understanding, and hang on every word uttered from her lips. He will keep her secure financially and spiritually, and she will always look at him as the rock of her life. He will help around the house and expect nothing of her when she is exhausted.

One of the great problems in marriage occurs after the first few weeks, when we realize that there is something wrong with those lists of expectations. That's when the trouble begins. None of us likes to have his dreams dashed.

On one occasion when our children were very small they asked, "Dad, will you take us to the circus Tuesday night?" Not wanting to appear cruel and insensitive, I said, "Maybe." Which to their minds was "Yes." If you ever become a parent, know that anything short of an absolute, nonnegotiable, white-knuckled, teeth-clenched "No!" is still a possibility. I said, "Maybe," and forgot about it.

I still remember coming home that Tuesday night. The kids were all excited. "Dad's home! Tonight's the night!" "What's tonight?" I said. "The circus! Remember?" "Oh," I said, "we're not going to the circus." They said, "OK. No problem," and danced off merrily to do something else. Not a chance. They were crushed.

Broken expectations are a leading source of discouragement and despondency. The most instructive passage I know about expectations is in Philippians 1. It is the report that Paul files with the church in Philippi about his time in Rome. In this report he notes that he is imprisoned (v. 13), that some of the Roman believers are envious and spiteful toward him (v. 15), and that Nero may decree that his life be taken (vv. 19, 21-24).

He has the makings for a lot of discouragement.

What fascinates me is that in the midst of this trial of expectations, he is victorious and ecstatic. How? The answer is given in verse 20: "[It is] my earnest expectation and hope, that I shall not be put to shame in anything, but that with all boldness, Christ shall even now, as always, be exalted in my body, whether by life or by death."

Paul had one expectation in life. It was not to continue to track as a premier apostle. Nor was it to be well liked by brothers and sisters in Christ. It was not even to be given a longer life in which to serve Christ. Those were not his expectations. His one expectation was that Christ be magnified through him. He sought to demonstrate the quality, character, and agenda of Christ *regardless of his situation in life.*

Rejecting comfort, pleasure, health, wealth, and peace as our primary expectations in life, and placing a reflection of Christ through us as the priority expectation will not only direct us toward His glory but help us bypass much trouble.

What can we expect from trouble? We can expect trouble to reveal ourselves as we really are and to come in at least seven different forms.

We can also expect trouble to elicit a response. The pivotal issue is what kind of response it will be. Progress toward grace, growth, and glory rises or falls on how we choose to respond.

5

Counting It Joy
The Strategic Response

If trouble is inevitable—and it is—then the other inevitability is that we will indeed respond to it.

But *how* will we respond? We can respond passively, fearfully, inwardly, assertively, philosophically, manipulatively—when trouble interrupts us, there are a host of options.

Out of all those responses one rises to the top. That strategic response is vital if we are to make it through. It is, in fact, nonnegotiable in realizing growth in character and competency and in bringing glory to His reputation.

It is the commitment to respond to trouble by "counting it all joy!"

Through our brokenness and tears, our hearts insist: *Impossible!*

Yet it is both possible and, when applied, productive. In fact, resisting this choice will derail progress and deepen despair.

THE NECESSITY FOR CONTROLLING OUR RESPONSE

When James writes, "Consider it pure joy, my brothers, when you encounter various trials" (James 1:2), he is referring to an arena we can control. The timing, depth, complexity, and duration of trouble is for the most part beyond our control. What is in our control is the way we respond.

One summer a few years ago at a major Bible conference a lady approached me after I had spoken during the Wednesday evening service. She remarked that she had been coming to the conference for many years and had always enjoyed the depth and the wisdom the great teachers of the Word of God who spoke there had brought to her life. Then she remarked that almost all of the speakers at that year's conference seemed so young. She asked me, "Where are the great seasoned statesmen of the faith that normally are at this conference?" It was one of those questions you don't know how to answer, so I just stood there. After an awkward pause, she went on to say, "Well, I'm disappointed. Quite frankly the ministry's not been much this week."

Now the "response" ball was in my court. What would I do? It's amazing how creative our responses are when somebody has shredded us on the spot. I do not remember exactly what I said, but I muttered something about feeling badly that she had not enjoyed the conference speakers and that I hoped that before the week was out there would be something God would give her.

A few other things I might have said went through my mind as I talked to her. But by God's grace, I chose to attempt to be understanding and kind.

Had I chosen to be defensive or hostile or in some other way repay her for what I thought was an insensitive and cutting comment, I probably would regret to this day that I had responded like that.

An important goal in trouble is to respond in a way that minimizes long-term regrets. I recall standing by the casket with the parents of a son who had died in his twenties. I heard them say something that made a marked impression on my heart. They said, "We've not always been perfect parents, but we have no regrets. We enjoyed our life with him and he enjoyed his relationship with us." What a wonderful commentary to come to the end of a relationship and to realize that while it wasn't perfect, there are no regrets.

THE RESULT OF A RIGHT RESPONSE

Right responses in the midst of trouble always minimize regrets. One of the primary goals in moving through trouble successfully is to go through it in a way that you can look back and realize that you did your best to respond properly and are not ashamed of how you managed the aspects that were in your control.

The story of Judas in Scripture is a fascinating and instructive tale of a life of wrong responses that ended up in the depths of regret.

Being the most trusted disciple in the group, he was given the responsibility of being treasurer. So trusted was he that when Christ dipped the sop and handed it to Judas in response to Peter's question about who was to betray Him none of the disciples at the meal understood who Christ meant. They thought that when Judas left the room after having received the sop he was going to buy something for the work. It never crossed their minds that Judas was the one who would betray Christ. Yet John tells us that underneath it all, Judas was addicted to greed and personal gain and that indeed he was a thief and would often steal from the treasury that he controlled (John 12:6). No doubt his dreams were that when Christ established His kingdom he would be the treasurer and and ultimately become a wealthy man.

Interestingly enough, it was right after Jesus Christ announced that He was going to the cross and would not be establishing an earthly kingdom that Judas left the disciples and went and bartered the head of Christ for money. Thirty pieces of silver. It's as though he said to himself, "Now that my prospect of greater riches is gone, at least I can get thirty pieces of silver out of this deal."

What is more significant is that Judas was more committed to his own comfort and ease than he was committed to going through difficulty in his identification with Christ, as Christ predicted that all the disciples would.

Judas's option for what seemed to be the comfortable way out was a response that filled the remainder of his life with regret, regret so deep that he could not live with himself. Matthew reports that after Judas had betrayed Christ and "saw that Christ was condemned," his heart was filled with sorrow (Matthew 27:3).

Our response to a crisis will lead us
. . . to reap a harvest of regrets . . .
or . . . the joy of knowing that we
chose the biblically correct response.

My dad used to say to me, "Joe, the problem with you is money burns a hole in your pocket." Those thirty pieces of silver burned a hole in Judas's heart as they rattled in his bag. They became a symbol of his sorrow and a reminder of his regret. So deep was his regret that he went back to the Jewish leaders and threw the money at their feet. Then he went out and hanged himself. The response that had seemed the easiest, the most natural, and the most comfortable, that seemed to to be exactly right and appropriate ended up being the response that led Judas to the depths of despair.

As a pastor I've been through several building programs. Of the things I've learned through that experience, number one is that you let the decorating committee do what it wants to do. It's much easier that way. In one of my ministries, my secretary was bolder than I. The committee thought we ought to have blue carpeting throughout the office complex. She did not like or want blue carpeting. She went head to head with the decorating committee over the issue and finally won. Her office would have beige, earth tone on the floor. Just before the project was to be implemented, she walked into my office and said, "Pastor, I've decided to have blue carpeting in my office." I was shocked. She went on to say, "I realized last night that if I have my way on this carpeting, every time I walk into the office the carpet will be a reminder of my stubbornness."

Our response to a crisis will lead us either to reap a harvest of regrets that etch themselves on our minds as lifelong reminders of poor choices, or to reap the joy of knowing that we chose the biblically correct response. Though the crisis may have been painful, we have the privilege of knowing that through it all we did our best, that our conscience is clear. Regardless of the outcome, we did not do things that deepened our distress through accumulated symbols of sorrow.

Productive responses are the responses that are outlined in God's Word. In times of crisis we need to fight through the baggage of our feelings, instinctive responses, advice from well-meaning friends, and past response patterns to check in with the "boss" to see what He believes would be appropriate. Imagine being faced with a crisis and pausing—eyes glazed over a bit—only to hear someone ask, "What are you doing?" You respond, "Checking my biblical data bank to find out how to respond."

That's how the process begins.

THE JOY OF RESPONSE

How then should we respond? Although there are specific patterns of response in regard to issues like forgiveness, compassion, mercy, understanding, justice, and patience, one general command fits every case. It is God's command to *consider every trial to be a thing of joy.*

Initially, that seems unreasonable because trouble does not feel joyous. In fact, trouble and emotional joy are incompatible.

If we are to respond constructively, we must understand that the text does not tell us to *"feel* it a thing of joy." For that we can be thankful. It is impossible for us to manipulate our emotions. Emotions are a result of circumstances, body chemistry, how we have slept, what we have dreamed, or even what we may have eaten the night before. When I'm not feeling right about things, I don't have a joy button that I can press and suddenly feel wonderful. For the most part, emotions come and go, often dictated by circumstances of life, and although we are usually able to keep them in check, it is impossible to change them dramatically.

Emotions are the baggage that comes with our trouble. They were never intended to direct our response. They come along for the ride. The emotions we feel are legitimate and normal. Feeling guilty about feeling down is unnecessary and wrong. Even Jesus wept.

What is right, however, is that we cannot permit how we feel to dictate how we respond. If you have traveled through the mountains, you may have seen ramps for runaway trucks. They are for drivers who have lost their brakes and are dangerously careering down the road, out of control. At that point their trucks are driven by the weight of their baggage. It's disaster waiting to happen. Letting our emotions dictate our actions is like letting the baggage do the driving.

It is in our choices that our lives should be directed to a productive end.

When we understand what the word *consider* means, it becomes clear that James is speaking of a nonemotional choice in this text. Among other things, the word *consider* is an accounting term for reckoning items one to another. In fact, some Scripture versions use the word *reckon* in the place of *consider*. At any rate, it is clearly a word that deals with cognitive, mental, volitional activity as opposed to emotional feelings. The text requires that when pain penetrates my existence I need to immediately, *mentally,* reckon that pain to be a thing of ultimate joy.

Counting trouble a thing of joy does not require that we feel happy.

Since in the original language the word *consider* is used in accounting contexts, we can think of our minds as a ledger book with different columns we can use to record our response when difficulty crosses our path. Our response to difficulty might be to pick up the pencil of our mental notebook and put a check in the self-pity column, wondering why this has happened to me again and why I am always the one to have difficulty. So we throw a pity party for ourselves and wallow in the despair of "woe is me." That is one type of mental response.

There is another column that is often checked—the column of blame. We might try to figure out who is to blame for our problem—of course it is never us—and put a check in the blame column, as we seek to put off any feelings of personal responsibility for the mess we're in.

Or we may put a check in the column of revenge. I'm amazed at how creative we can be when it comes to carrying out revenge on others who have hurt us. There is a column for withdrawal. There is a life-is-unfair column. There are columns for bitterness and guilt—but there is also a column for joy. Scripture demands that we move all the way across the ledger page until we come to that column and mentally make the check mark that says that we believe that, in the hand of God, what has happened will ultimately be a cause for joy.

THE CONTENT OF OUR RESPONSE

James 1:2-5 points to the fact that this is not simple mental gymnastics or the power of positive thinking to get us through. This "joy" response has real content. The end of the passage makes clear that if we process pain correctly, it will, in the end, bring us to completion in terms of character and equip us to be completed in good works in the ongoing days of our lives. God will use our trouble to produce character and competency in our lives. That is the joy factor.

What the book of Hebrews says of Jesus and His suffering should not go without notice: "Let us fix our eyes on Jesus, . . . who for the joy set before him endured the cross" (Hebrews 12:2).

Counting trouble a thing of joy does not require that we feel happy about our difficulties but that we understand that ultimately and finally God's good hand will make the experience worthy of joyful praise and thanksgiving. This mental outlook keeps our focus not on the moment of pain but on the culmination of the process.

What enables us to respond positively? The joy response is fortified by what *we know* to be true in the midst of trouble.

Verse 3 speaks to the process of the joy response by saying, "Knowing this . . ." That statement directly ties our capacity to count our difficulty an ultimate thing of joy to what we know to be absolutely true. There is a tremendous advantage that the believer has in terms of facing trouble in terms of truth that is logged in his mind before the trouble comes. There are times when trouble puts us in such deep despair that our capacity to learn through it is almost nonexistent. Logging the right kind of knowledge in advance is greatly beneficial in light of the inevitability of tough times in our lives.

The success of the Persian Gulf War is likely attributable to the fact that our pilots were well trained before they actually faced battle. As one military commander observed, the generation raised on video games was able to take control of sophisticated equipment that required good eye-hand coordination and accurate timing. When the conflict came, they were well prepared in the skills it required.

What we know to be true . . . is the foundation upon which we can . . . go . . . to the column called joy.

Knowledge, whether learned in the midst of trouble or logged in advance, is that commodity that remains certain in the midst of changing emotions and circumstances. It is like an anchor firmly secured in bedrock that keeps the storm-tossed ship from being blown onto rocks.

One of my all-time favorite sports memories is of the final hockey game played in the 1980 Winter Olympics in Lake Placid, New York. Facing Scandinavian and Eastern Bloc teams composed of seasoned veterans who had given their lives to the state to prepare for and to compete in the Olympic matches, the American team, made up for the most part of amateur players from colleges and universities, seemed on paper to be no match. The Olympics came at a time when the spirit of Americans was at an all-time low. It seemed Americans had little to cheer about.

Yet the American team persisted and won game after game. I came home from church on the Sunday that our boys were playing the Russians and turned the television on and noted, much to my surprise, that though the match was more than half over, we were playing head to head with the Russians. I sat down and could hardly move. I watched with anxiety as our men skated, and flinched every time the Russians cocked their sticks to make a shot. I relaxed in relief when I saw that they hadn't scored. It was an agonizing, white-knuckled, tight-stomached spectator event for me and for many others who watched across the country. Then in the final moments it became obvious that we might beat the Russians. It seemed impossible. It seemed so wonderful. We at last had something to cheer about. We had done it.

That night after church, the network decided to replay the hockey game. We invited some friends over to enjoy the game with us. I sat back in my easy chair, a glass of Pepsi® in my hand and a bowl of popcorn on my lap. Relaxed, calm, and enjoying every moment of the very ^ame game. No whitened knuckles, no tight stomach. What made the difference?

What I knew.

What I knew to be true! The outcome was secure.

Though we don't know the final score in trouble, we do know that in God the outcome is secure. No matter what it is, it is unshakably scheduled for grace, growth, and glory.

What we know to be true, regardless of the trouble, is the foundation upon which we can accurately, reasonably, intelligently, and confidently go all the way across the ledger page until we get to the column called joy and confidently put a check in the appropriate place.

What is it that we can know to enable us to positively respond in trouble? We know that our trouble is guarded by His permission and guaranteed by His character and His presence. We know that He intends to turn it to our growth and His glory. We know that the damage Satan seeks to do us and God's reputation can be thwarted and denied by the choices we make.

Still, there is an even longer list of confidence-building, joy-assuring realities.

6

Truths That Hold Us Steady
God's Provision in the Storm

Pilots flying in a storm or in darkness quickly become disoriented and deceived by their senses. Pilots say that when they are flying without visibility, they can be flying in a tight circle while their senses assure them that they are flying straight ahead. When a pilot becomes disoriented in this way, his body is telling him one thing and his instruments are telling him something completely different. To keep flying safely, he must rely on the instruments in his plane. Those instruments will tell him what is actually and absolutely true.

What we know to be true in trouble is the instrument panel that provides certainty regardless of how we feel. Hurting people have often told me, "I know that is true from the neck up, but somehow it doesn't make sense in my heart." We assume that if it only makes sense in our heads, it's not helpful.

But it *is*.

Part of the process of working through pain is learning to hang onto what we have from the neck up. When our hearts are broken and hurt there won't seem to be a pipeline from the brain to the emotions. That's OK. Just don't let go of what you know. That's the key to making it in the midst of difficulty. That's exactly why God's Word says, "Consider it pure joy . . . because you *know* that . . . (James 1:2-3, italics added).

What can we know in the midst of trials? What are the reliable instruments that track us successfully in the midst of difficulty?

---

*If you are suffering through a trial
. . . find someone who has
been there before.*

In James 1:3-4, the stabilizing truth is that we can *know* that "the testing of [our] faith produces endurance" and that we should "let endurance have its perfect result, that [we] may be perfect and complete, lacking in nothing" (NASB). James is saying that we can know that pain is a *process with a purpose*. That specific piece of knowledge will enable us to implement the joy response.

There are at least six mental anchors in Scripture that give stability in the midst of trouble.

COMMONALITY

Three of those "knowable" truths are found in 1 Corinthians 10:13. The first portion of that verse reads, "No temptation has seized you except what is common to man." Unfortunately, we tend to think of the word *temptation* only in regard to sin. Although that is a part of its meaning, limiting the term to sin greatly reduces the scope of the verse. It is interesting to note that the word *temptation* is from the same word group we find in James 1:2 (italics added): "Consider it pure joy, my brothers, whenever you face *trials* of many kinds." Actually 1 Corinthians 10:13 could read, "No *trouble* has seized you except what is common to man."

This portion of verse 13 provides the first principle we need to rely on in the face of problems. It is the principle of commonality. You can be absolutely sure that you are not the only one who has gone through this kind of problem. You haven't been singled out by God to be the one individual in the history of the human race selected to experience a situation like this. There were others before you, and there will be others after you.

It is said that misery loves company. What is true is that "misery *needs* company" to keep us from terrible aloneness, to enable us to find others who have struggled against the same dragons, and to prepare us to help others who are yet to be ambushed.

In the American church we have privileges that few other believers around the world have. One of them is good Christian literature. Most Christian bookstores today have available much good material about people who have walked through dark times—biographies of suffering heroes, specific titles on sudden tragedy, abuse, broken homes, disappointments, and a variety of other problems.

If you are suffering through a trial, you should be able to find someone who has been there before, who has struggled and come to know grace, growth, and glory. Networking with others as a point of support and insight can be very helpful. Look for heroes who have made it through with their hands held high in victory. What you're suffering is common to others.

And as God, by His grace and in His time, begins to put the pieces of your growth and His glory together, you can fulfill the truth of commonality by becoming a support to someone else who is looking and listening for that "Can I help? I've been there too!"

A tremendous frustration for me as a pastor was to stand with people who were experiencing terrible pain. I learned early on that I should not say, "I understand." That was because I *didn't* understand. I had never been there myself.

But then some special person who *had* been there before would walk up and put his arm around this suffering soldier and say, "I understand. Let's talk."

BEARABILITY

The second reality is the truth of bearability. First Corinthians 10:13 goes on to say, "And God is faithful; he will not let you be tempted beyond what you can bear." That statement guarantees that God never gives us anything more than what we can bear. It's like the country road that has a sign posted before a bridge, "Load Limit 5 Tons." God, who knows our "load limit," limits the load He permits us to carry.

I like to thank God for the things He did for me today that I am unaware of.

One of the states in which we lived had a bottle return policy. Each empty pop bottle was worth ten cents. Neither Martie nor I especially liked to take the bottles back, which meant that they accumulated in our garage, leaving a veritable savings account in pop bottles. One evening when the stacks of bottles had got intolerably high, I decided to take them back. Our then preschooler son, Matthew, followed me into the garage and nobly said, "Daddy, let me help!" (Why is it that when children are too young to help they want to help you, and when they finally get old enough to be constructive they aren't interested?) "Sure, Matt," was my reply. This precious little boy took two cartons of bottles and struggled to get them into the car.

Off we went to the grocery store. I got a grocery cart and piled the bottles in, put some under my arms, and started to the store. Matt had his two cartons. Halfway across the parking lot he set his down, looked at me, and exhaustedly said, "Daddy, I can't do it. They're too heavy." I replied, "Listen, Matthew. You started the project; you wanted to help. Now buck up and do it right. Pick those bottles up. I'll count to five."

Do you think I said that?

Not a chance! As a father I understood his limits. I picked up Matt's cartons and put them into the grocery cart. If this earthly, fallen father would do that for his child, how much more will my Father in heaven, who intimately knows me, be willing never, ever to permit anything more than what I can bear. You can know that. If He permits it to come into your life, it's bearable.

It is not that our trouble does not often seem unbearable. It often does. It is that we can know if God has permitted it, in His intimate knowledge of who we are—and He knows us better than we know ourselves—we can be assured that it is indeed not beyond our capacity.

In this guarantee is the promise that though we may be bent, we will never be broken.

Our lives only become brittle and fatally broken when, by poor responses, we permit bitterness to add additional weight to the load of our struggle. There is a particularly strategic side to this principle that we dare not miss. All of us have had the feeling at times that God really hasn't done anything for us in a long, long time. We see Him at work for others, yet much of our life seems strangely lacking in terms of the supernatural. We tend to sour and think that, though God may be at work somewhere, "He's not at work in *my* life!"

Actually, if God did nothing more than redeem me, He's already done far more for me than I deserve. That is reason enough to give Him praise and glory for the rest of my life. Yet beyond that, He is active every day in my life as He stands as the sentinel at the gate of my existence, weighing, measuring, and excluding everything that exceeds my load limit. Those are the things I know nothing about. Periodically, as I fall asleep, I like to thank God for the things He did for me today that I am unaware of. When there is nothing on your thanksgiving list, thank Him that He has guaranteed that the struggle is bearable and has kept from you things that would have been crushing blows.

SUPERNATURAL OPTIONS

The third reality we can know for sure is that God has supernatural options available for delivering us from trouble. The closing portion of 1 Corinthians 10:13 says, "But when you are tempted, he will also provide a way out so that you can stand up under it." I love 2 Peter 2:9: "The Lord knows how to rescue godly men from trials." It guarantees that when I get into trouble, though I may feel as though I am trapped in a room with four walls closing in on me and no windows or doors for escape, God already knows how He is going to deliver me. He is in the business of making ways of escape.

When David, being hunted by Saul, ended up in a cold cave, he cried out to God, "How long, O Lord? Wilt you forget me forever? How long will you hide your face from me? How long must I wrestle with my thoughts and every day have sorrow in my heart? How long will my enemy triumph over me?" (Psalm 13:1-2).

We, like David, feeling God has forgotten, are prone to plan our own escape. We say, "I know what I'll do. I'll—no, that won't work. Here's what I'll do—no, I don't think that will work either." It's the total despair of seeming to be locked in with no way out.

The children of Israel, finally delivered from Egypt through God's performance of phenomenal miracles, now stand with their backs to the Red Sea and see the dust of the approaching Egyptian host on the horizon. Their response? "God has options we never dreamed of in Egypt. Remember those ten plagues? We never dreamed God would deliver us like that. Can you imagine what He is going to do now? This is going to be spectacular."

Unfortunately not.

They said, "We would rather be slaves in Egypt than die out here."

Yet God had a plan to deliver them that they never would have dreamed of. God said to Moses, "Why are you crying out to me? Tell the Israelites to move on. Raise your staff and stretch out your hand over the sea to divide the water so that the Israelites can go through the sea on dry ground" (Exodus 14:15-16). We know the rest of the story. The sea parts, and the Israelites walk across. The Egyptian army follows, God closes the sea, and they sink like stones. God's people are free. The trouble is past.

God knows how to deliver the righteous from trouble.

I recall counseling a lady who had just come to know Christ. She was interested in becoming God's kind of woman, so we were studying passages of Scripture that had to do with what a biblical wife is like, and we were talking about the whole matter of gracious cooperation with her husband's leadership. She came to me one day and said, "Pastor, I've got a major problem. I have been saving up my money for a dining room suite. I love the one my mother-in-law has and am looking for something just like it. After I've gone through the used furniture ads in the paper, my husband and I drive around and look at them. My husband is so insensitive.

He doesn't seem to be real interested, and we've been to a couple of places where I really liked them, and he says, "No, I don't like those.'"

I encouraged her to be patient and wait for the Lord to work in His way. The next week she came back and said it was worse. She said, "The worst thing about it is that it's my money and he could care less what kind of furniture we have in the house. He doesn't know if we have French Provincial or 'Early Salvation Army.' He's basically interested in his newspaper, easy chair, and the TV."

A couple of weeks later she came back and said, "You're not going to believe this, but my mother-in-law called me and said that she had bought a brand new dining room set and wanted to know if I wanted hers."

God does not always work exactly like that. But it is clear that He has lots of different options of deliverance. When we are faithful and patient through trouble, God will, in His time, exercise options of deliverance that are far beyond what we ever dreamed.

God's Power

The fourth truth that we know is that God's power is at work in our difficulty. I have a friend who has one of these wonderfully engineered cars. When we come to a light and wait for it to change, I feel like telling him, "Start the car." It sits there with no vibration or noise from the engine. If I had that car, I'd probably break ten dozen starters thinking it had gone dead. If it weren't for the tachometer sitting at idling RPMs, you'd think the power was gone. In trouble, much of the time we do not notice God's power engineering the trouble toward resolution. Sometimes we see very little evidence of the work of His power. Yet His power *is* busy at work in at least three dimensions.

Dimension number one is the claim of Romans 8:28, where we are assured of God's power to bring that which is bad to that which is good. It's His phenomenal ability to take the worst possible circumstances and transform them and ultimately bring good out of that which is terrible. If you ever get really disappointed or discouraged, read the story of Joseph. Betrayed by the people closest to him, his own family, he was sold into Egypt as a slave. Rising to a place of influence in Potiphar's house, Joseph daily faced Potiphar's wife's efforts to seduce him.

We experience emotional liberation from our enemies when we say, "God, they are Your business. You deal with them."

The Egyptians prided themselves on beautiful, sensual women. Potiphar, being one of the leading bureaucrats in the land, no doubt had a wife who was rather spectacular. He's off on business much of the time, she's no doubt lonely, and Joseph, who is young and strong, is running the household every day. She grabs him, and he runs. I say, "From whence come men like that?" How righteous can you get? God looks down on Joseph and says, "Joseph, nice going. You're My kind of man! . . . Three years in the slammer." For three years nobody remembers him. In those years God may very well have been extracting the arrogance from his life. Then, in His time, God delivers Joseph and elevates him to the second highest position in the empire.

There's a famine in the land and his treacherous brothers come for food. Now their lives are in his hands. In time, Joseph's father, who has moved to Egypt, dies, and the brothers are fearful that Joseph will kill them in revenge. They come cowering before Joseph, only to hear him say, "Don't be afraid. Am I in the place of God? You intended to harm me, but God intended it for good to accomplish what is being done, the saving of many lives" (Genesis 50:19-20). God had used His power to turn the very worst moments of Joseph's life into that which was good.

This capacity of God to bring good out of evil was demonstrated in the cross. Was there ever a moment in the history of humanity that was so brutal, unfair, and personally agonizing than the moment when the Son of God was hung as a criminal? All of hell rejoiced for three days. Satan had won the day. He had exterminated the conquering Son. Then God spoke to the grave and turned that which was incredibly bad into that which was wonderfully good. Redemption from sin. Hell canceled and heaven gained.

Unfortunately, unwilling to wait patiently, we often get in the way by attempting to take the project into our own hands, and while God is trying to do His good work, we're down here messing up His project with vengeance, bitterness, and other counterproductive responses. We need to walk in Christ's footsteps, who "'committed no sin, and no deceit was found in his mouth.' When they hurled their insults at him, he did not retaliate; when he suffered, he made no threats. Instead, he entrusted himself to him who judges justly" (1 Peter 2:22-23).

The second kind of power at work in the midst of trouble is God's power to deal with our enemies. Joseph said to his brothers, "Am I in the place of God?" (Genesis 50:19). That is a very important statement. Romans 12:17 instructs, "Do not repay anyone evil for evil. Be careful to do what is right in the eyes of everybody." The wonderful truth of this was demonstrated when Joseph admitted he had no business getting back at them, that God is the one who carries out justice. We experience emotional liberation from our enemies when we say, "God, they are Your business. You deal with them." We are then released to be like God and love our enemy in return. Romans 12:20-21 reads:

> Do not take revenge, my friends, but leave room for God's wrath, for it is written: "It is mine to avenge; I will repay," says the Lord. On the contrary:
>
> "If your enemy is hungry, feed him;
>   if he is thirsty, give him something to drink.
> In doing this, you will heap burning coals
>   on his head."
>
> Do not be overcome by evil, but overcome evil with good.

It is liberating to know that God will deal with those who cause trouble in my life. That releases me to love them. Jesus said,

> You have heard that it was said, "Love your neighbor and hate your enemy." But I tell you: Love your enemies and pray for those who persecute you, that you may be sons of your Father in heaven. He causes his sun to rise on the evil and the good, and sends rain on the righteous and the unrighteous. If you love those who love you, what reward will you get? Are not even the tax collectors doing that? And if you greet only your brothers, what are you doing more than others? Do not even pagans do that? Be perfect, therefore, as your heavenly Father is perfect. (Matthew. 5:44-48)

Again, our problem is that we get in the way. God has not equipped us or given us the capacity to deal justice and vengeance to our enemies. That's why it always gets messed up when I try. He is the only one that has that right and the power and wisdom to do it well.

I'll never forget an older lady who came to my office and heatedly dumped on me a long list of objections about her husband. I asked how long she had been married. It was more than forty years. I have never in my life, nor would I ever, counsel anyone to break up a home. But as she went on and on about how miserable he was I finally said, "Why have you lived with him so long if he's so bad? Did you ever think about just checking out? I'm not advising it, but I'd like to know what you think." She said, "Oh, no! I'd never walk out of this marriage."

I thought that was an honorable attitude until she continued. It was evident that she hated him so much that walking out of the marriage would have meant that she couldn't torment him anymore. For her, that was a reason for staying. Why would you want to give up the opportunity to shred your enemy at every turn?

God has called us to a better way. In the midst of trouble, we can count on the power of God to deal with those who are against us. And we are then free to be like our Father in heaven, free to bless those who curse us, to pray for those who spitefully use us, and to love our enemies, because the power of God will ultimately deal justly with them.

The third kind of power we can count on is found in 2 Corinthians 4:7: "But we have this treasure in jars of clay to show that this all-surpassing power is from God and not from us. We are hard pressed on every side, but not crushed; perplexed, but not in despair; persecuted, but not abandoned; struck down, but not destroyed." I love knowing that God values the preciousness of my being. Though I may go to the edge, in His wonderful, sovereign power He will always keep me sane and safe as I respond properly to Him and to the trial.

The psalmist often says that God holds us with His right hand. The "right hand of God" is an Old Testament metaphor for strength. Have you ever walked with one of your children, holding his hand? I don't know what it is, but somehow a child can be walking along beside you, and all of a sudden his legs just fly out from under him—for no reason at all. But though he is off balance and in danger of falling, his parent's power keeps him from "destruction."

Is there a problem that is bigger than the reservoir of God's grace? The answer is no.

What a wonderful picture. God holds me with His powerful right hand as I walk the sidewalk of life. If I trip and both feet go out, it's OK because He is holding me. We can count on His power to ultimately and finally protect us and keep us from complete destruction.

GOD'S DIVINE SUPPORT

The fifth truth we can affirm in difficult times is the reality of God's divine support. Second Corinthians 12:9 tells of Paul's struggles with his thorn in the flesh. He prayed three times to be relieved from it, but to no avail. So he submitted to the lifelong affliction and, with a positive spirit, resolved to let God's strength be made strong in his weakness, discovering that God's grace was sufficient to support him through the trial.

In my seventeen years in the pastorate, I have stood by people who have endured phenomenal suffering and trouble. And I have to tell you, a lot of times I walk away and say, "I can't believe how well they're doing." I think if that were me, I would be a basket case. Then I hear Paul's confidence ringing in my heart,

"God's grace is sufficient." Like the everlasting arms, God's grace comes under us and wraps around us. It overtakes us, and we are supported.

His grace is His unmerited help to us. In trouble, it will be there. How much? Is there a problem that is bigger than the reservoir of God's grace? The answer is no. That's why Paul said, "God's grace is sufficient."

A PROCESS WITH A PURPOSE

The sixth principle we can count on during times of trouble is that God uses trouble as a process with a purpose in our lives. God never wastes our sorrows. Any pain He permits is to be used by Him as a process with a purpose.

When trials put us on public display, it is our privilege...
to turn the tables on Satan's attempt to deface God's glory.

There are two biblical purposes: *our growth,* which is what James 1:2-4 speaks of, and *God's glory* (John 9:3). Trouble attracts the attention of people around us. Hebrews 10:33 says, "Partly, whilst ye were made a gazingstock both by reproaches and afflictions; and partly, whilst ye became companions of them that were so used" (KJV). One Christmas somebody gave one of our children a plastic fireman's hat. It was one of those gifts you wished they hadn't given. It had a red plastic flashing light on top of it and a battery-operated siren. Our kids ran all over the house with this siren and light going. You couldn't help but notice their presence.

It's like that with trouble. As soon as trouble hits our lives, the lights start going off and everybody starts watching us. That's why it's such a wonderful opportunity to process the trial in the biblical manner so that as a "gazingstock" in trouble, with the world watching, we can demonstrate the presence and power of God in our lives. Trouble becomes a platform for God's opportunity to glorify Himself and show Himself strong.

Recently I sat in the audience at Moody Bible Institute's Founder's Week and listened and watched as Joni Eareckson Tada told of her deep love for her God and her joy in Christ.

She was paralyzed from the shoulders down, but her face literally beamed as she sat in her wheelchair. It was clear that God was real, satisfying, fulfilling, and enabling in the midst of her lifelong trial. It was a credible statement to the reality and power of God and His grace. Whereas remorse, self-pity, and bitterness are the products of nonbiblical responses to suffering, the evidence in her life of God's power and presence revealed through her pain was an unimpeachable statement of the grace and glory of God.

Suffering is a platform for the display of God's power. Sometimes that power is displayed by His miraculous deliverance, and sometimes it is displayed by the grace He gives to positively endure as we reflect forgiveness and peace during an ongoing, sometimes lifelong, problem.

When trials put us on public display, it is our privilege through biblical responses to turn the tables on Satan's attempt to deface God's glory and through our troubles to demonstrate clearly His worthiness to be worshiped, regardless; to give Him our willing allegiance, regardless; and to demonstrate the reality of His presence, power, and peace in the midst of pain.

Not only is pain a process with the purpose of demonstrating God's glory, but it is also a process that focuses on the purpose of enabling our growth in character and in competency for living. James 1:2-4 states that we should count it all joy, knowing that the process will contribute to a life that is becoming "mature and complete, not lacking anything."

How does that happen? The text goes on to speak of the four-step process that leads to our growth—the testing of our faith, our endurance, our yieldedness, and our reliance on prayer.

The testing of our faith comes when trouble puts our faith to the test. Trouble calls faith to the witness stand. What is faith? Faith is our unflinching reliance on God. I'm glad that God is not a slippery commodity who slides out of our hands or a moving target in whom we cannot trust. God doesn't play hide and seek with us. He has revealed His Word, His promises, and His ways to us. They are reliable, solid, and clearly true. They do not change. These are the handles that we cling to in trouble.

When trouble comes, by faith I cling to His *promises.* "Never will I leave you; never will I forsake you" (Hebrews 13:5). "And we know that in all things God works for the good of those who love him, who have been called according to his purpose" (Romans 8:28). "Perseverance must finish its work so that you may be mature and complete, not lacking anything" (James 1:4). Even when there's no light at the end of the tunnel, when you are in a deepening darkness, and your heart is broken, these promises are true and will provide your source of stability.

When trouble comes, by faith I cling to His *ways.* "Heavenly Father, I know what You've done in the past and how You have responded in real lives in Scripture. Since that's the kind of God You are, I'll hang on to You through this. I will not become bitter or manipulative. I will simply permit You to do Your work in Your time," and by faith we hang onto that.

When trouble comes, by faith I cling to His *charac-ter*. First Corinthians 10:13 says, "God is faithful." By faith we hang onto the fact that God will be faithful. He's not going to show up at the end of your trouble and say, "I'm really sorry, but I've had a busy three weeks. I just couldn't quite get around to your situation." It's not going to be like that. His character is firm and reliable, fully worthy of our confidence. God is loving, just (that helps in terms of our enemies), righteous, gracious, and merciful.

When troubles come, our faith is tested. It is called to the witness stand to demonstrate whether or not we will believe and nonnegotiably apply His promises, ways, and character to every situation of life. When we give in to lesser responses, it is a reflection of the strength of our faith.

We are surrounded by a great
cloud of witnesses, ...
some who have suffered greatly.
... And now it's our turn.

The testing of our endurance comes about when we apply the "faith response" to our situation. If we cling tenaciously to God, we won't give up or give in. Interestingly, the English word *endurance* is made up of two Greek words, *hupo* and *meno*. *Hupo* means "un-der"; *meno* means "to remain." Endurance is the ca-pacity to remain under the stress until God's work is done.

Our family loves to eat watermelon. Our children realized early on that if you put your thumb on a wet watermelon seed and apply a little pressure, it will spurt out and go flying across the table. It is especially fun if you can score a bull's-eye on your sister.

A lot of us respond to trouble in the same way. Life begins pressing on us, and what is our response? *Get me out of here! Lord, solve this problem. Immediately.* But when God says no, instead of trying to wiggle out, by faith we claim God, hang on by faith, and hang in there as faith produces endurance. Staying under the pressure with a good spirit is an important part of the divine process as He works toward His productive end in our lives.

In times of trouble, isolate specific aspects that are true about God and list them with the passages that guarantee the truth. Memorizing and praying through those sections of Scripture will be helpful in anchoring them in your heart and mind. A pledge to wait for God to fulfill those truths in your life while you unflinchingly obey and trust Him is the essence of endurance. Look with anticipation for grace, growth, and glory, and rejoice in any signal that the process is working in your life. Regularly check your commitment. Have you started trusting in yourself and your own ways? Have you become manipulative, resentful, bitter, cutting, unforgiving? What checks are you putting in what columns? Are you by faith clinging to God and responding in a biblical way?

After exercising unflinching faith in Him and persisting, the third dynamic is to *yield to the process.* "Consider it all joy, my brethren, when you encounter various trials, knowing that the testing of your faith produces endurance. And *let* endurance have its perfect result, that you may be perfect and complete, lacking in nothing" (James 1:2-4, NASB; italics added).

"And *let* endurance have its perfect result" is the command in the text. It's like surgery. When the surgeon comes in and says we need an operation, we say, "OK, I'll endure the process and take the pain." We have confidence in the surgeon and believe that it's ultimately for good. So we are wheeled into the operating room and the anesthesiologist approaches the table as the doctor walks in. We watch as he walks past the trays of razor-sharp knives and the nurse puts his gloves on him. They roll the tray with the knives on it toward the operating table, and we mutter under our breath, "No way," and bolt off the table as the doctor grabs a knife and tries to operate as he chases us around the operating room.

Obviously not.

Yet many of us give God that kind of trouble when He seeks to produce growth and glory through a trial in our lives. That's why verse 4 requires that we yield to the process. We must resist the initial impulse to jump off the table. We need, instead, to place unwavering faith in the divine surgeon and endure, knowing that ultimately it will culminate in a way that we can claim joy and praise for the process.

Last, James tells us to *pray*. Verse 5 says, "If any of you lacks wisdom, he should ask God." There will be plenty of times that you don't know what to do or how to respond. Go to the Father and seek wisdom from Him. If you are so distressed that you cannot pray or don't know how to pray, Romans 8:26 assures you that the Holy Spirit takes the groanings you cannot even utter and brings them before the Father, untangles all their confusion, and lays them before Him on your behalf in accord with His will.

Prayer in the midst of trouble helps us see God again. It gets our eyes off our problems and focuses us afresh on God, who is all-powerful, merciful, and just.

Prayer reveals to me things about myself. When I pray in the midst of trouble, I may say, "Lord, you know this mess with Bob and Sally? Well, they . . ." and it is often that the Lord interrupts and says, "Yes, I know about them. But can we talk about you?" Prayer has a way of revealing things in my own life that need to be faced if I am to become "mature and complete, not lacking anything." I find that God regularly responds, "I'll take care of them. Let's talk about you."

In prayer I am often reminded of biblical principles that are relevant and true. In prayer His Word starts coming back to me. I am reminded of passages and principles I need to apply. This is wisdom from God. Wisdom about Him, wisdom about me, wisdom about His Word. "If any of you lacks wisdom, let him ask of God."

There is never an easy way to go through trouble, but there is always a right way—by counting it joy because of what we know to be true about the process, by exercising faith, by yielding to the process, and by praying for wisdom.

When our oldest son, Joe, was quite young, Martie and I thought it would be a good thing for him to learn to swim. We signed him up for lessons at the YWCA. On the first day, Martie packed his bag and I took him off to his lesson. We walked down to the men's locker room and slid his little bathing suit on. He stood there straight as a ramrod. As I looked at him I could almost see the gold medal swinging from his neck.

I sent him out the door to the pool and went to the room at the end of the pool where parents sat and watched the lessons. I got there just as my son got to the end of the pool where all the other children were. My son took one look at the instructor, one look at the pool, and backed up against the wall and began to cry. What made it worse was that the instructor turned to the parents' room and pointed to my son as if to say, "Whose child is this?" I thought, *I've fathered a coward.* I met little Joe back in the locker room as he poured out his heart to me in urgent tones between sobs and gasps for breath. This was probably the biggest problem he'd ever faced. A full-fledged trial.

"Daddy, I'm scared. I don't want to do this."

I said, "It's important that you learn to swim. When you get old and become a daddy, you may have a little boy. Someday you may be out fishing together and if your little boy falls out of the boat, you'll need to know how to swim to rescue him." It seemed like good logic to me.

"I don't care! Don't want to. I don't want to learn how to swim," was his response.

We worked it through, and finally I said, "I'll tell you what. You need to believe me that this is important. It's part of being prepared for life. I'll come to every lesson and be in that little room, and any time you're scared, you look up at me and I'll flash you the 'OK' sign and that will remind you that it's important and that your dad has a purpose."

So off he went. As I went into the room, he took one look at me, I signaled the agreed-to sign, and his lessons were well launched. The day came that he had to put his face in the water. I'll never forget his standing in the water with all the other children, water right up to his chin. They started going down the line, bobbing their faces in the water like champs, and it was getting closer to being Joe's turn. He looked at the water and looked up at me. I was flashing the sign and motioning, "You can do it! You can do it!" Splash! Down went his head—and as he came up he looked up at me as I proudly formed the OK sign and mouthed, "You did it! Nice going, Joe!"

What got him through? He had faith in his father that there was purpose in the trouble. He kept his eyes fixed on the one who promised to help him through.

Hebrews 12:1-3 says that we are surrounded by a great cloud of witnesses, people who have gone before us, some who suffered greatly (Hebrews 11:32-40). And now it's our turn. We take the baton and face the arena of life, which is a veritable obstacle course with the ad-

versary at every turn, seeking somehow to discredit
God and destroy us. As we start our run through this
fallen place, the "cloud of witnesses" cheers us on. Peter, crucified upside down because he refused to be
killed like his Savior. John the Baptist, beheaded. And
they're cheering us on, saying, "You can do it! Run the
race! Take your turn!"

In every Roman arena there was an emperor's box.
Every athlete looked to see if the emperor was there on
the day of his race. And, as the text says, we, too, look to
Jesus, "the author and perfecter of our faith." And as
we do, He lifts His nail-scarred hand and flashes the signal, guaranteeing grace, growth, and glory, and He says,
"You can do it! You have not yet striven unto the shedding of your own blood."

As Scripture states,

> since we are surrounded by such a great cloud of wit-
> nesses, let us throw off everything that hinders and the
> sin that so easily entangles, and let us run with perse-
> verance the race marked out for us. Let us fix our eyes
> on Jesus, the author and perfecter of our faith, who for
> the joy set before him endured the cross, scorning its
> shame, and sat down at the right hand of the throne of
> God. Consider him who endured such opposition from
> sinful men, so that you will not grow weary and lose
> heart. (Hebrews 12:1-3)

Being committed to the fact that difficulties are a
process with a purpose requires that our purposes for
life be like His purposes for us. If our purpose in life is
to be comfortable, well-liked, happy, and accumulating
enough money to buy the things we want, then we will
never find hope in trouble. These are not God's driving
agendas for our existence. Character is more important
to God than cash, convenience, or comfort. Our competency is of greater value to Him than simply going

through life blissfully, yet unprepared and functionally unable to make a contribution to people's lives and to the cause of eternity.

The measure of how productive trials have been in our lives is how much more we are like Jesus Christ now than we were when the trouble began. Pain is a process with a divine purpose, and God never wastes our sorrows.

Among all the question marks that invade our hearts and heads in times of troubles, the certainties revolve around the answer to Who? and What?

Who? It is God and me. The reliable, trustworthy God working in me and through me with an outpouring of His grace until my growth and His glory are realized.

What? My knowledge of what is clearly true and reliable. Choosing to bypass alternate, unproductive, and destructive responses, we choose to reckon it ultimately to be a thing of joy in His powerful and creative hand. Choosing to not permit the baggage of our feelings to drive our responses, we direct our reactions by what we know to be true, counting it all to be a thing of joy as we cling by faith to what is true about Him: His promises, His character, and His ways; yielding to the process; praying for wisdom and enduring under the pressure until there is measurable growth in both character and competency and a reflection of His glory.

The issues of *growth* and *glory* are often demonstrated in Scripture. The penetrating theme of the New Testament is that God will do what is necessary to bring us to the likeness of His Son. His purpose may be to "grow" us to be capable and usable by using problems to reduce the risks that we bring to the kingdom. Growth may be fostered by the difficulty that finally forces us to be God-sufficient rather than self-sufficient. And His glory through us will only become evident as we seek to turn every attack of the adversary to a clear testimony of God's worth and works in us and through us.

7

The Purpose of Bringing About What Is Good

"Conforming Us to the Likeness of Christ"

Surgery.

Many of us have experienced it. It is inconvenient, painful, unpleasant, frightening, and disruptive. Yet, we choose to submit to it. Why? Because the pain is worth the gain. It promises to produce a "good" result.

God's Word assures us that, for the believer, all pain is a process with a purpose. In fact, God guarantees the purpose to be a good outcome for both God and the one going through the trial.

> And we know that in all things God works for the good of those who love him, who have been called according to His purpose. For those God foreknew he also predestined to be conformed to the likeness of his Son, that he might be the firstborn among many brothers. (Romans 8:28-29)

BALANCING THE GUARANTEE

Two issues must be dealt with in the face of this familiar passage.

First, God does not intend for us to become spiritual masochists who think that progress comes only in pain and that there is no productivity in pleasure and success. Granted, it is tough to be productive in good times. In times of pleasure and prosperity, self-sufficiency and pride may rob us of an awareness of our need for God and of our need to change.

There really is an "Easy Street" in Honolulu, Hawaii. Interestingly, it is a "Dead End" street. Yet properly viewed, God's positive blessings can be a motivation to growth and glory as well. Realizing how undeserving we are and how gracious He has been in abundant provision should strike a depth of gratitude that motivates us to deeper love, loyalty, and service. That is why God affirms that *all* things work together for good (Romans 8:28).

> *Our resource in pain is not what we feel, but rather what we know.*

Pleasure, success, and good things are as significant as suffering. We must learn with Paul the "secret of being content in any and every situation, whether well fed or hungry, whether living in plenty or in want [for we] can do everything through him who gives [us] strength" (Philippians 4:12-13). Let us never forget that it is God who "richly provides us with everything for our enjoyment" (1 Timothy 6:17). Our assurance is that whether in pleasure or in pain, God is able to bring about that which is good as we respond constructively.

Second, we are prone to become shallow and flippant with a guarantee like this. In the midst of heavy hurt, it's easy for us to come alongside and say, "Well, brother, remember Romans 8:28." I stopped my casual use of the verbal panacea for all our ills the day I received this letter.

> Dear Pastor Stowell:
> I've thought of communicating with you on your current sermon theme (Romans 8:28). Since August, every time that theme comes up, I am painfully reminded of my brother's death by suicide.
> He left a widow with two small daughters. I had to identify him for the coroner and tell my parents what had happened. Then I had to clean the walls and ceiling and furniture of his blood and flesh, as he had shot himself in the head. The legacy of his death confronts us on a regular basis.
> I have asked myself often—what good was there in his death—to us—or to him? There is no answer.
> Except for a handful of close personal friends, the local church was not much comfort. Most acted as though it never happened.

How do you make Romans 8:28-29 make sense to a hurting friend like this? The guarantee of Romans 8:28-29 contains three truths that fortify us in difficulty.

Go with What You Know

Trouble brings with it a bucketful of emotions. Despair, hurt, revenge, self-pity, anger, sorrow, and a dozen other feelings. If we are not careful, those feelings can dominate us and disorient us from what we know. Emotions derail our thoughts and detour our commitments. How we feel tends to distort what we know.

Our resource in pain is not what we feel, but rather what we know. When Romans 8:28 begins with the words "And we know," it literally means that we have an absolute knowledge. Our knowledge in pain is not a hope so or maybe or might be—but a know so reality.

While our emotions are like quicksand, knowledge is bedrock.

Notice that each major section on difficulty in Scripture begins with an appeal to what we know. "We also rejoice in our sufferings, because we know that suffering produces perseverance; perseverance, character; and character, hope" (Romans 5:3-4). As we have seen, James 1:2-4 directs us to "consider it pure joy . . . whenever you face trials of many kinds, because you *know* that the testing of your faith develops perseverance. Perseverance must finish its work so that you may be mature and complete, not lacking anything" (italics added). When our emotions jade our perspectives, God's truth doesn't change. Truth is truth regardless of how we feel.

God is working all things to be good.

God's truth gives us a unique edge to which we can cling in trouble.

What do we know? We have learned that with God there is the victorious, overcoming work of grace, growth, and glory through difficulty, that in trouble there are certainties to which we can cling: the certainty of His goodness, creative power, justice, holiness, and total knowledge. We know that He is a God of accurate timing, consistent presence, certain purpose, unfailing love, and productive empathy. We know that He must always relate to us in the context of those truths.

We know that trouble develops character (Romans 5:3-5) and that trials equip us to be more useful (James 1:2-5). Because of Romans 8:28, we know that good is the ultimate purpose of the process of pain. Knowing and clinging to what we know makes the difference. Truth is our stability factor in trouble.

A friend was telling me about devastating months of depression that she had gone through. Nothing had seemed to help. She told me that the only thing that kept her from breaking was "the truth that heaven is real." That basic bit of knowledge kept her head above the swirling flood of her emotional despair.

Another friend, whose child had died two months before, told me, "It hurts more now than it did then. All we have is the fact that God is so sovereign and omniscient," he said as his voice broke. That's pretty basic, but it was enough to get him through.

As God's people we have the advantage of truth in pain. It's a definite edge in trouble. It's our resource. Cling to it.

PAIN IS A PROCESS

Romans 8:28 goes on to remind us that pain is a process toward an ultimate good. Foundational to the acceptance of pain is the awareness that God has us in process. None of us is what God wants us to be. Though God loves and accepts us the way we are, He sees all that we can become. Pleasure has a way of making us very satisfied with ourselves. Pain catches out attention so that God can process us into His dream for our lives.

That process is defined in several dimensions. First, it is all-encompassing. Since God works in *all* things, we are guaranteed that whatever He permits—whether pain or pleasure, bane or blessing—He is able to use it all to process us.

Beautiful automobiles are especially alluring. They become beautiful and useful through a process. The process involves a design concept that is reached through bending, banging, shaping, heating, riveting, fusing, and tightening. It is a slow process as the assembly line moves at an almost imperceptible speed, but it is a certain process with a desirable goal. Hundreds of component parts make up the whole. Some are unsightly and added under great pressure, whereas others beautify; yet each is essential to the process.

The truth that pain is a part of God's process is seen in the context (Romans 8:18, 23, 26). To wish to be processed by God except for the "pain" part of it is to be a hunk of shapeless steel that wishes to be a beautiful and useful commodity without the process.

Not only is God's process all-encompassing, but we also know from Romans 8:28 that it is a continuous process. "God works" is a present, continuous tense verb. God will never abandon His purpose for us or the process to accomplish it.

I have many unfinished projects in my basement. Things I tore apart to restore. Antiques that I have begun to refinish. With God I am never an abandoned project.

The third dimension to this all-encompassing, continuous process is the most significant of all. It is the reality that this is a divinely supervised process. Note that Romans 8:28 says, "God works." Behind the scenes of my life story is the hand of God. Moving, changing, limiting, applying pressure, providing strength, rearranging. God is the one working all things to be good.

Auguste Bartholdi went from France to Egypt in 1856. He was awestruck by the grandeur of the pyramids, the magnitude of the mighty Nile, and the beauty of the stately Sphinx of the desert. His artistic mind was stimulated. While on this trip he met another visitor to Egypt, Ferdinand de Lesseps. Ferdinand was there to sell an idea. An idea to cut a canal from the Red Sea to the Mediterranean Sea that would save merchant ships the long journey around the tip of the African continent. Auguste was taken by the concept. He decided to design a lighthouse to stand at the entrance to this canal.

It wouldn't be an ordinary lighthouse. It would symbolize the light of Western civilization flowing to the

East. It took ten years to build the Suez Canal. For ten years Auguste worked on his idea. He drew plans, made clay models. He scrapped plan after plan. Then he had the right one. It was the perfect design.

Only one problem remained. Who would pay for it? He looked everywhere, but no one was interested. The Suez Canal was opened—without a lighthouse. Auguste went back to France defeated. Ten years of toil and effort wasted.

You would have liked his idea. It was a colossal robed lady that stood taller than the Sphinx in the desert. She held the books of justice in one hand and a torch lifted high in the other to light the entrance to the canal.

After Auguste returned to France, the French government sought his artistic services to design a gift to America. The Statue of Liberty lighting the New York harbor demonstrates that what happens in the midst of disappointments can often be a prelude to good things beyond our imagination.

In the end, the puzzle is
something that makes sense
. . . a good thing of beauty.

If, in the normal course of life, things that seem to be disappointing, difficult, and defeating can be processed into that which is magnificent and significant, how much surer is this process with the hand of our wise and powerful God guaranteeing the outcome.

We must take caution, however, against slipping into an irresponsible fatalism that sees God as both the source and the processor of pain. Within the "all things" of Romans 8:28 are the reality of human choices and consequences.

In her book *Affliction* Edith Schaeffer tells of a child who fell off a cliff to his death and of another who slipped through the ice into a frozen lake. Did God push the child from the cliff? Did God push the boy through the ice? No, these tragedies occurred because we live in a fallen place and are a part of a fallen race. It was a choice to venture too close to the edge of the cliff. A choice not to check the safety of the ice. But it is the powerful, creative hand of God that takes these tragic settings of life and works them all to good regardless.

Life is a lot like a jigsaw puzzle. Often our lives can seem like a thousand pieces spilled onto the table. Our lives seem to be confused, disoriented, senseless, and tragic, but then God comes and carefully, wisely, in His way and in His time, puts the pieces together. In the end, the puzzle is something that makes sense ... a good thing of beauty. That's what we know.

As Paul affirmed, "He who began a good work in you will carry it on to completion until the day of Christ Jesus" (Philippians 1:6).

PAIN—A PROCESS WITH A PURPOSE

The third dynamic is that God has no process without purpose. The guarantee of Romans 8:28 states that we know that God processes in us all things toward good. That's His purpose. For the believer, there is no pain without purpose of a good result.

I stood in the church foyer and said to a set of relieved parents, "God has certainly been good to spare you your son." The night before, their son had been in a terrible auto accident. He was rushed to a hospital more than an hour away for special treatment. All night he hung onto life by a thread. He had made it!

Standing next to his parents was another couple whose daughter had been killed in a car wreck a few years before. It was then that it hit me. *Had God not*

been good to them? What was I saying about my defini-
tion of good? What must my comment have meant to
the parents who were less fortunate?

God defines *good* for us in Romans 8:29. The text
says that this process is for those who have been called
according to God's purpose. What is God's purpose?
According to verse 29 it is to conform us to the image of
His Son, and that is good. Anything that will bring us to
a more accurate reflection of the quality of Christ in and
through our lives is good. Whatever it takes, pain or
pleasure, is good if it conforms us to His likeness. That's
God's goal in the process of pain. He takes all that He
permits and makes it a part of the process to bring us to
reflect the image of Christ.

God . . . has the power to complete the project.

Our family was at a conference some time ago and
Matthew, our youngest child, fell and broke his wrist. I
have never seen anything like it. His arm took a sharp
left at his wrist and then turned again to resume its normal journey to his hand. It was grotesque.

We rushed Matthew to the hospital where the doctor began to set his wrist. I watched as the doctor pulled
and twisted Matthew's arm. The doctor began to per-
spire, and I felt like jumping up and pulling the doctor
off my son. But I simply sat and watched. I knew that
Matt's arm needed to be restored to its original design
and purpose. But pain and several weeks of inconven-
ience would be a part of the process.

We, too, broken and hurt by sin and self-will, must
often be reset by a good and loving God. Set back to His
intended purpose, the image of His Son. Set back to a

heart of compassion, righteousness, and love. Set into the original purpose of His glory through us.

God not only has the intention of processing us to what is good, but He also has the power to complete the project. I love what the prophet Isaiah said when he wrote that God would "comfort all who mourn; to appoint unto them that mourn in Zion, to give unto them beauty for ashes, the oil of joy for mourning, the garment of praise for the spirit of heaviness; that they might be called trees of righteousness, the planting of the Lord, that He might be glorified" (Isaiah 61:2b-3, KJV). He is able to restore the years that the locusts have eaten (Joel 2:25).

Michelangelo carved the sculpture *David* out of a hunk of stone. Other artists take colored oils and canvass and create masterpieces. Beams of steel are bent and welded to create monuments to who knows what in our city squares. But I have never seen an artist even attempt to make something beautiful from ashes. Only God can do that (Isaiah 61:3).

God is able to bring the love of Christ into our lives. It may take some brokenness. It may require that we go through a time of need to become sensitized to the needs of others. If it requires pain to do that, then it is good.

Can we weep with those who weep? God may need to stain our cheeks with tears so that we can genuinely empathize as Christ does.

Are we self-sufficient? The tragedy of our affluent culture is that we rarely sense we *need* God, when in reality we desperately do. God may need to strip away some of our security, as painful as that may be, to conform us to the God-sufficiency that Christ displayed; that would be good.

Are we faithless? It may take the impact of a tragedy for us to experience the reality of God that we may learn to lean on and trust Him as Christ did; that would be good.

Are we proud, indifferent, carnal, selfish, unforgiving, negative, or angry? God has something better. The lifestyle of His Son.

God is able to effect positive change in us. He knows what is best. He knows what it takes. He will, as the loving, all-powerful sculptor, chip away until Jesus is seen in the hardened hunk of our lives.

For those of us who know God, pain is a process with a certain purpose. We don't make it through tough times. We are made through tough times—made into the beauty of Christ Jesus.

And that is good.

8

Capable and Usable
Reducing the Risk

Our newspaper recently carried a story about a clergyman who was not only liberal theologically, but sociologically as well. His sermons regularly carried the theme of the goodness of everyone. Only environments were evil. He sided against the police and often cried out about their brutality. He supported laws that favored the rights of the criminal over the rights of the victim. He often cast his lot with the American Civil Liberties Union in their social action endeavors. Needless to say, his views were a source of consternation to the old-timers in his flock.

A week before this clergyman was scheduled to speak to his church's senior citizens group, he was mugged by hoodlums, who robbed and beat him mercilessly. He was injured and shaken, both emotionally and philosophically. He nearly canceled the engagement, but then thought better of it and showed up in bandages and a sling.

As he began his speech, he told how the mugging had caused him to rethink his social positions. He admitted that he had been shaken to the core. Yet, to the group's surprise, he said that, in spite of it, he had decided that he would not let that violent episode change his views or his theology. He would go on preaching as he always had. Shocked, a woman in the last row stood up and shouted, "Mug him again!"

WHO NEEDS TO BE CHANGED?

Who needs to be changed? We do.

It's amusing how we go through life feeling that everyone else ought to change—and we know just how it should be done. We act as though we are God's appointed agents of change. It never seems to cross our minds that God may wish to change *us*.

With four years of seminary study in my pocket, I walked into my first ministry with an agenda as long as my arm. I thought, *I'm here to change this place.* It soon became clear that God would use it to change me.

The board members in that first church loved me, but they kept my feet to the fire in administrative details. I needed to know how to work with lay leadership, how to be careful in my work, how to dream with others. I needed to develop those skills so that I would be capable and usable in the days ahead. As unpleasant as it was at the time, it was God's change agent in my life.

Then I assumed that I was ready. Competent. Usable.

I took my next pastorate. I asked all the right questions. I knew everything that should be changed. I could see exactly why God had led me there. Boot camp was behind me. It was *my* turn to be the agent of change. I walked in, ready to go—and it was as though God said, "Mug him again."

I often wonder how many times God will have to "mug me" before His message gets through. Before I change my mind to think as He thinks. Before He has me in a form and place that I am usable in a maximum way in His kingdom work.

I hasten to say that God really does not mug us. But He does encounter us on the streets of our existence to bring about change in our lives. To change us so that He might use us.

I'm glad God is not finished with me yet. It gives me a sense of confidence to know He cares enough for me to continue to shape, mold, mend, and stretch me. I want to be useful to Him. Though it sometimes hurts, the pain is worth the gain. It is His goal to change us into instruments "useful to the Master and prepared to do any good work" (2 Timothy 2:21).

How do you make a shepherd boy a man of military might and skill? You send him to boot camp for ten years, where he becomes an instant general to a growing band of men.

CAPABLE AND USABLE

It's hard for us to imagine what happened in this little shepherd boy's heart the day the great prophet of Israel came to his house, passed by all his older brothers, and anointed him as the next king of Israel. If I promised my sons that some day they would play for the world champion Detroit Tigers, they would never forget it. All their years of development would be filled with that anticipation. Multiply that feeling and perhaps you can understand what being king meant to David.

More special yet is that it all began to come true. David was invited to play his harp for King Saul. He became fast friends with Jonathan, the king's son. The women of Israel sang his praises. David was often at the king's house. It all made sense. Someday soon God would make *him* king.

Then in a rage Saul hurled a spear at him, and David fled. He was now a fugitive, running for his life. For ten years David ran, hiding in caves with a band of loyal men. Desperate and deserted, he cried,

> How long, 0 Lord? Will You forget me forever?
> How long will You hide Your face from me?
> How long must I wrestle with my thoughts
>   and every day have sorrow in my heart?
> How long will my enemy triumph over me?
>
> Look on me and answer, 0 Lord my God.
>   Give light to my eyes, or I will sleep in death;
> my enemy will say, "I have overcome him,"
>   and my foes will rejoice when I fall.
>   (Psalm 13:1-4)

The heavens were deafeningly silent.

God needed David to be a warrior, a man of military might and skill. He would lead God's people in conquering Israel's enemies. He would make way for the next king, Solomon, a king of peace, to build the Temple.

How do you make a shepherd boy a man of military might and skill? You send him to boot camp for ten years, where he becomes an instant general to a growing band of men. David learned the terrain intimately and knew every cave and corner of the topography. Most important, he learned that God was his protector and provider.

As David fled from Saul, his time of trial endeared him to all of Israel. He protected the people's flocks and kept their land safe from Philistine marauders (1 Samuel 25). That developed into a coast-to-coast popularity for David. A grass-roots support for him to become king.

Six hundred men gathered themselves to David, men who were the dregs of society (23:13). "All those who were in distress or in debt or discontented gathered around [David], and he became their leader" (22:2).

How do you take a lonely shepherd boy and make him a leader and manager of men? Give him ten years with six hundred unusual men. Then he will be ready to manage the people of Israel.

David was righteous, but not ready. For David, this ten-year ordeal was an extended trial. But for God, it was just long enough to make David capable and usable.

Why does God want to change us? Isn't God satisfied with us the way we are? No. He accepts us as we are, but He is not satisfied until we are usable for Him.

A few weeks ago I went to the store to buy a new garage door opener. I shopped, found the right one, paid for it, and took it home. It came in two boxes. I unboxed it, assembled it, hung it, and wired it. In the process, there was a lot of banging on its parts to get them to fit. A lot of tightening of its screws and bolts.

God runs a phenomenal risk when He entrusts His work and reputation to us.

It's like that with God. He accepts us just the way we are. But He then wants to make us usable. He may need to take us out of our comfortable, neatly packaged boxes. Bang on us. Tighten here and loosen there. Whatever it takes.

If we are to be successful in pain, it is essential that God's goals become our goals. If it is our goal to be conformed to the image of His Son—to be righteous, to find our sufficiency in Him, to serve Him with the risk reduced, to be made capable and usable—then we will willingly endure whatever leads us to the goal. We will realize that the pain is worth the gain. If, however, our goal is to be happy, healthy, wealthy, and comfortable, then we will resist the trials of life and become bitter and brittle in the Master's hand. We must agree with God at the outset. Our prayer should be, "Lord, I want to be capable and usable for You. Whatever it takes, I am ready. Only go with me."

Part of being capable and usable for Him is to be sure that our attitudes are usable. Two dangerous and disabling attitudes are pride and self-sufficiency. God will often use trials to transform our pride to humble reliance and our self-sufficiency to a usable God-sufficiency.

RISK REDUCTION

Risk reduction is not uncommon to us. We take extensive measures to protect things precious to us. We are willing to take phenomenal steps to reduce the risks to our lives, health, money, friends, power, and prestige.

Soon after the "Tylenol" deaths in the early 1980s, the makers of Tylenol marketed the pills in tamper-proof, sealed bottles marked in plain view with this statement: DO NOT USE IF THE SEAL IS BROKEN. Laws force us to use seat belts. Exorbitant amounts of money are paid for insurance against theft or loss. Home security systems are installed. We enroll in self-defense courses. We eat right and get enough sleep to guard our health. All of this to reduce risk.

God runs a phenomenal risk when He entrusts His work and reputation to us. His reputation in this world is largely seen through those of us who claim to be His children. Yet we are prone to bouts of pride, selfishness, moral impurity, jealousy, anger, and a host of other problems. As the stewards of God's kingdom work, we are risks to Him. He trusts us to train the next generation for His glory. He trusts us with the proclamation of the great oracles of His truth. He has committed to us the financial support of the ministry of Christ's kingdom. The spreading of the good news to a lost world has been placed in our hands.

Trusting all of this to us is indeed risky business. God must feel somewhat as my friend did when he gave his daughter in marriage. His daughter was a well-mannered, beautiful young woman. When the groom-to-be came to ask for her hand, my friend admitted that he felt like he was handing over a priceless Stradivarius violin to a two-hundred-pound gorilla.

Is it any wonder that God seeks to reduce the risk of His work through us?

INSECURITY

Insecure?

I would have never guessed it of him. He is a well-known communicator, an effective teacher of the Word. And now he was telling his congregation that he often feels insecure. I was surprised, but I could identify with the feeling.

A thorn is anything that reduces self and resurrects the power of Christ.

I, too, find insecurity a frequent companion. It gnaws at me and internally humbles me. It plagues my heart with questions. Did I preach an effective sermon? Was I misunderstood? Will that special person accept me for what I am? What am I doing here? Shouldn't I be better as a father? Am I as sensitive as I should be to my wife?

To be straightforward, I dislike insecure feelings intensely. But as much as I dislike their intrusion into my life, I realize that they have tremendous value. Value to God and value to my productivity for Him. When I am feeling insecure, my heart flies to the Lord for strength. I seek Him for perspective; I search His Word for comfort. Not only does insecurity keep me close to God, but it keeps me from the distortion of a proud spirit. It reminds me of how truly insufficient I am in and of myself. It reminds me of how much I need God. My insecurities make me sensitive to others.

The truth is that I am a risk to God's effective work through me. Pride, insensitivity, self-sufficiency and a host of other potential risks lurk under the surface of my life.

Pride chokes productivity by alienating those whom God wants to reach. Pride leaves the door of life open to many failures. A door through which lying, moral impurity, stubbornness, anger, and vengeance can walk. I know as well that self-sufficiency assumes that the works of God are a credit to our human abilities. That leaves me nonproductive and vulnerable to glorying in myself. Pride tends to ignore the needs of others who hurt and leads me to a selfish perspective on life.

My insecurity serves to reduce the risk of pride, self-sufficiency, and insensitivity. It works to turn pride into authentic humility, self-sufficiency into a trust in God to be sufficient for me, and my insensitivity into a useful and empathetic sensitivity to others.

I have come to realize that insecurity is a thorn to live with. Yet a thorn reduces the risk to God's work through me and contributes to a productive usefulness to Christ.

Thorns in the Flesh

Second Corinthians 12:7-10 outlines for us the productivity of Paul's risk-reducing thorn. Paul relates the problem, purpose, and proper response to the pain of thorns:

To keep me from becoming conceited because of these surpassingly great revelations, there was given me a thorn in my flesh, a messenger of Satan, to torment me. Three times I pleaded with the Lord to take it away from me. But He said to me, "My grace is sufficient for you, for My power is made perfect in weakness." Therefore I will boast all the more gladly about my weaknesses, so that Christ's power may rest on me. That is why, for Christ's sake, I delight in weaknesses, in insults, in hardships, in persecutions, in difficulties. For when I am weak, then I am strong. (2 Corinthians 12:7-10)

Initially, Paul *recognized his vulnerability.* He knew that pride could be a problem for him. He had been the object of God's special attention. God had shared phenomenal revelations with him, revelations not trusted to anyone else (vv. 1-6). He realized that this could lead to a distortion of his self-perception and that his heart could become conceited.

Arrogance is a tremendous barrier to our effectiveness for God. How open are you to arrogant people? Have you ever listened to a proud man attempt to teach you the Word? I find that when I discern a spirit of pride I am tempted to block the teacher out. Self-exaltation is a risk. It distorts and blocks God's work through us. Paul was wise enough to perceive that his difficulty reduced the risk of pride.

What was Paul's risk reducer? Scripture does not tell us. Paul simply indicates that it was a difficulty sent by Satan that was a permanent and troubling condition. The Greek word for thorn, *skolops,* means "a pointed stake." This was a problem of major proportions and was like a stake driven into his body. Paul was constantly aware of its presence.

Thorns come in many shapes and sizes. A thorn could be something *physical,* as it might have been for Paul. A sickness. A bodily limitation. Or it could be something *emotional.* An insecurity that keeps you close to the Savior. Charles Haddon Spurgeon, London's greatest preacher of the last generation, often felt heavy weights of despondency that deepened his sensitivity to Christ and the crises of others. It may be the feeling of sorrow that lingers from a past sin and keeps you from committing it again.

A thorn might be *circumstantial*. A businessman was recently sharing how there seemed to be little possibility of a promotion for him in his company. He related how frustrating that was for him until he realized that it was of God. He shared that he was intense and aggressive in his work and that he had a struggle with materialism. "I'd sell my soul to the company if I was moving up quickly. God has done this to focus my attention on the priorities of my family and my relationship to the Lord. He keeps me from the danger of making my business, money, and things a god in my life."

A thorn could be something *social*, perhaps a person—an in-law or a headstrong child. God has always seen fit to periodically place in my life someone who has been uniquely used of Him to reduce the risk of carelessness, slothfulness, and pride.

Actually, a thorn in the flesh can be any trouble that reduces the risk in me to hinder God's effective work through me. It is anything that refines me and keeps me sharp for His glory. Anything that keeps pride, arrogance, self-sufficiency, immorality, or any other lust of the flesh in check so that God's strength can work without my getting in the way. A thorn is anything that reduces self and resurrects the power of Christ.

Responding to Thorns

Paul's thorn was a messenger of Satan. That rings true to our earlier discussion, in which Satan was affirmed as the primary source of pain. It thrills me to watch God turn Satan's best efforts to defeat us into usefulness for His glory. God can always use for glory what Satan intends for abuse. The key to that victory is our response.

We can respond by letting the thorn fester to produce a discouragement that leads to bitterness, anger, self-pity, and defeat. Or we can look at our pain from God's point of view and discover its usefulness. Paul's four responses are the keys to his thorn's becoming productive in his life.

First, Paul sought *release* (2 Corinthians 12:8). He prayed, pleaded with the Lord three times to take the thorn away. It is not to our spiritual credit to want to experience pain. Even Christ asked the Father three times to remove the cup of His suffering. That's where Paul began. He did the most he could to seek release, and God answered his prayer. But God's answer was no. In certain circumstances, pain is more productive than release. It was that way for Paul.

When God said no, Paul adjusted. Thorns in the flesh are a lot like stones in your shoes. If you can't get them out, you adjust to them. Though the adjustment may take some time, it is absolutely critical to using your thorns productively.

After seeking release, Paul adjusted by *tapping the resource*—God's grace (v. 9). Grace is God's help to us when we do not deserve it, when we cannot help ourselves. God's grace is available to us through several channels.

God's Word is one source of help in trouble. His Word provides comfort, proper mental orientation, promise, and purpose. "If Your Law had not been my delight, I would have perished in my affliction" (Psalm 119:92). A lady sat in my office and told me of her recent crisis. It was terribly complex and confusing. It left her full of despair. Few of us could identify with the magnitude of her problem. She said, "Pastor, there have been times when I have lost all support from around me. Times when I felt disoriented and totally alone in my confusion. In those times, all I had was the strength of the Word of God. It was my only stability. The only mark on the compass of my life, my only point of hope and orientation. Pastor, I've made it this far because God's Word is there and God's Word is true." She had experienced God's grace through the strength and comfort of Scripture.

God's grace also comes through prayer. Hebrews 4:16 says, "Let us then approach the throne of grace with confidence, so that we may receive mercy and find grace to help us in our time of need." This kind of praying is more than "Now I lay me down to sleep," or, "Thanks for the food," or "Give me what I want." This kind of praying stays before God's throne, agonizing, if necessary, till the grace breaks through. The grace of prayer may be a settling peace that comes over your spirit. It may be God's reminder of a specific promise to which you can cling. As you talk with God, you may be reminded of His mercy, His power to turn that which seems bad into that which is good, His loving care, or any other of a dozen qualities of our God. Prayer changes our perspective in times of trouble and blesses us with the grace to bear up victoriously.

Pastor, God has made me small
and bent over so that I can be
right down where children are!

Grace also comes to those who reject pride and take a humble posture in pain. "God opposes the proud but gives grace to the humble" (1 Peter 5:5). Who are the proud in pain? They are those who demand comfort and ease. Those who think they deserve better. They are those who say, "God, not *me!*" Those who say, "I'll do it alone, Lord, if You don't mind. I'll make it through this by myself." Pride chokes off the grace that the humble receive.

The humble, like Christ, say, "Yet not as I will, but as You will" (Matthew 26:39). The humble submit to thorns instead of resisting them. They are the ones who receive the grace of God.

God says that grace also comes through the words of those around us. "Do not let any unwholesome talk come out of your mouths, but only what is helpful for building others up according to their needs, that it may benefit [literally, "give grace to"] those who listen" (Ephesians 4:29). The carefully chosen words of those in the family of God are a source of God's grace. A word of encouragement. A word of strength. A word of God's perspective. A word of understanding. "A word aptly spoken is like apples of gold in settings of silver" (Proverbs 25:11).

After being denied release, and adjusting by tapping the source of grace, Paul *realized the purpose of this thorn in his life.* He realized that God's "power is made perfect in weakness" (2 Corinthians 12:9). Paul's thorn prevented him from developing a spirit of pride and arrogance; therefore, his thorn enabled God's power to be full and unhindered. The risk had been reduced and God's work was maximized!

Finally, Paul *responded with gladness and delight* (2 Corinthians 12:9-10). Paul wanted nothing less than for Christ to be strong through him. If it took trouble to accomplish that goal, then Paul would rejoice in the trouble. He knew that his thorn was a companion to keep his life eternally productive. "For Christ's sake, I delight in weaknesses, in insults, in hardships, in persecutions, in difficulties. For when I am weak, then I am strong" (v. 10).

Upon visiting a church, we took our son Matthew to his Sunday school class. A small, bent-over lady met us with a glowing smile and a warm welcome for Matthew. Later, Matthew excitedly told us about what he had learned and what songs his class had sung. We were impressed with the unusual effectiveness of that teacher.

I was soon to become the pastor of that church. I marveled often at this widow's positive spirit. It was contagious. I'll never forget the day she shared her secret with me. She said, "Pastor, God has made me small and bent over so that I can be right down where children are! I love them so much, and if I weren't like this, I couldn't relate to them so well." She had turned her thorn into triumph. It was the key to her usefulness. It had become a blessing and she rejoiced in it.

God's working through us is risky business. If it takes a thorn for Him to be effective and productive in our lives, then let us tap the grace, realize the purpose, and rejoice.

9

God-Sufficient
Taking the Trouble to Get to Know Him

Recently a friend asked if the affluence of many in our church was a problem. My guess was that he suspected that a lot of them were caught up in materialism and in striving for gain. Though that may be true for some, that's not our worst problem. Our struggle with affluence is that we lose sight of how much we need God.

Knowing that we need Him easily and quickly gets lost in the fact that we have all we need. Clothes, food, safety, security, friendship, and fun are all available and affordable.

Assuming that we have provided it all for ourselves, we become self-sufficient. Self-sufficiency is a problem in that it takes our relationship with God from one of reliance to one of mere ritual. When we cease to perceive how much we need God, He soon fades out of sight, then out of mind, then out of life.

Americans live in an affluent and all-providing culture. If we can't afford something, we buy it on credit. If we are poor, we rely on government aid. We have our

health, houses, families, jobs, friends, and heritage.
Who needs God?

In *The Problem of Pain* C. S. Lewis wrote, "Everyone has noticed how hard it is to turn our thoughts to
God when everything is going well. The statement, 'we
have all we want,' is a terrible statement if that all does
not include God." He goes on to cite St. Augustine, who
said, "God wants to give us something, but He cannot.
Our hands are full and there is nowhere to put anything."

The tragedy of this self-sufficiency is that we end
up placing our trust in our money, family, job, income,
friends, and our own ingenuity as though they will last
forever. Yet they are all fleeting; each could be gone in a
moment. God is the only steady, daily, eternal reality
that is sufficient for all our needs and wants.

THE JEOPARDY OF SELF-SUFFICIENCY

Self-sufficiency distorts our responses to life.
When our sufficiency is in earthly things, we are tempted to manipulate, intimidate, or compromise our righteousness to maintain our sense of security in these
fleeting commodities.

Self-sufficiency leads to pride and self-glory which,
as we know, are repulsive to God. Christ reflects this in
His reproof to the church at Laodicea. "You say, 'I am
rich; I have acquired wealth and do not need a thing.'
But you do not realize that you are wretched, pitiful,
poor, blind and naked" (Revelation 3:17).

Self-sufficiency leads as well to idolatry. We end
up worshiping those things that provide our sufficiency
and security. If that source is not God, then we will
cease to worship God. Whatever the false source of our
sufficiency may be—whether it be a husband, a wife, a
child, a job, a brilliant mind, good health, or happiness—it will soon take first place in our lives.

God, knowing that self-sufficiency turns to pride, self-glory, and idolatry, warned Israel about their entrance into the Promised Land.

> When the Lord your God brings you into the land He swore to your fathers, to Abraham, Isaac and Jacob, to give you—a land with large, flourishing cities you did not build, houses filled with all kinds of good things you did not provide, wells you did not dig, and vineyards and olive groves you did not plant—then when you eat and are satisfied, be careful that you do not forget the Lord, who brought you out of Egypt, out of the land of slavery. (Deuteronomy 6:10-12).

Sure enough, the Israelites went into the land of plenty and forgot the Lord.

As with them, the only way the Lord can accomplish a sense of God-sufficiency is to strip away the layers of our self-sufficiency.

That stripping may be painful.

Let me tell you about a self-sufficient woman. She worked for a wealthy couple. They saw to it that she had all she needed—clothes, food, and security. She had a son. He was the joy of her life. She had heard about God, but she didn't *need* Him. He was little more than a word in her vocabulary.

Suddenly, difficulty stripped her life of *everything*. All she had was gone. All, that is, but God. She had no choice but to look to Him and learn of His central place in her life.

COMING TO THE END OF OURSELVES

That story is Hagar's. It begins in Genesis 16 when she bears a son to Abraham. Hagar is the head maidservant of Sarah, Abraham's wife. According to cultural custom, if there was no heir through the wife, the chief woman servant was to bear the heir. Hagar did, and named her son Ishmael.

Then the problems began. Expelled once from her home because of Sarah's anger, Hagar was met by God, who sent her back. In time, God opened Sarah's womb, and she bore the legitimate heir of God's promises to Abraham. As brothers are prone to do, Ishmael taunted and mocked young Isaac. Sarah, seeing her son being mocked, demanded that Abraham get rid of Ishmael and Hagar.

Note that Hagar's difficulty was not self-induced. In fact, she was a victim of Abraham and Sarah's scheme. Since Hagar was a slave, she had no choice but to bear Abraham's child. Later, she was a victim of her son's behavior. Finally, she was a victim of Abraham's decision. While she was simply doing her duty and living life responsibly, Hagar's life fell apart.

> *Hagar needed a firsthand experience with God. She needed to know . . . that God loved her and . . . could be her sufficiency.*

More significantly, Hagar's difficulty was God-ordained. God said to Abraham, "Do not be so distressed about the boy and your maidservant. Listen to whatever Sarah tells you, because it is through Isaac that your offspring will be reckoned" (Genesis 21:12). God did not ordain Hagar's difficulty because He didn't care about servants and loved Sarah best. God always has a fair, just, and good reason for what He ordains, even though the reasons were beyond Hagar's comprehension.

God ordained Hagar's trouble because God's Messiah seed was in jeopardy. God had promised that the seed of the woman would someday strike a fatal blow to the domain of Satan (Genesis 3:15). That promise was renewed to Abraham, and Isaac would carry on the Messiah seed. The story of Cain and Abel demonstrated that Satan would do all he could to extinguish the righteous seed that might fulfill God's promise and threaten his existence. Lest the story of Cain and Abel be repeated at that point in history, God sovereignly intervened. Isaac and Ishmael were separated to secure the safety of the messianic promise to Isaac. That separation not only served the purposes of God's messianic plan, but it was used by God to accomplish a significant work in Hagar's life as well.

Victimized by circumstances in a problem ordained by God, Hagar now saw her life go from bad to worse. Stripped away were her privileges as the chief maidservant—her fine garments, her food, her security, and her health. All that she had was reduced to a boy, some bread, a bottle, and a wilderness.

God was in the process of removing the layers of Hagar's self-sufficiency. Some of us can identify. Hagar lost her *purpose* in life (Genesis 21:14). She went from a maidservant to a nomad, from the caretaker of a wealthy estate to a manager of dwindling provisions.

Hagar lost her *provisions* for life (21:15). Soon the water and the bread were spent; thirst and hunger replaced them.

Hagar lost her *prized possession* (21:16). There was only one thing that was of deep personal worth to Hagar—her son, Ishmael. She now abandoned him because she could not bear the agony of watching him die.

Walking in Hagar's shoes helps us sense her helpless despair as she rations out the last few sips of water as they pass her lips under the intense heat of the sun. Think of her agony at losing the glory of her past position, security, and comfort. Watch as the young boy grows weaker in the wilderness, a boy not yet hardened to the rigors of life. Weakening, failing, groaning in pain, dying.

Hagar has lost everything. She has come to the end of herself.

We can't help but wonder, "Where is God?" Is His hand withered that He cannot help? Is His heart hardened that He will not weep with her? Are His ears deaf that He cannot hear her cries? Is He there? Would He ordain a difficulty that would waste and destroy?

AT THE END OF OURSELVES . . . GOD

Hagar's setting is by God's design. He has designed that the layers of *her* sufficiency be stripped away so that He might rebuild her life with *His* sufficiency. When Hagar comes to the end of herself, God is there.

Hagar needed a firsthand experience with God. She needed to know the reality that God loved *her* and would supply for *her*; that He could be *her* sufficiency.

At best, Hagar had a secondhand relationship with God. Though God briefly met her in Genesis 16:7-13, she primarily knew God as the God of Abraham and Sarah. She had watched *their* God work for *them* and supply miraculously for *them*. Their God would now become her God. Dramatically, He would personalize Himself to her. It required, first, that she be taken to the end of herself so that God could prove His sufficiency.

He provides Hagar with a personal experience with *God's Word.*

> God heard the boy crying, and the angel of God called to Hagar from heaven and said to her, "What is the matter, Hagar? Do not be afraid; God has heard the boy crying as he lies there. Lift the boy up and take him by the hand, for I will make him into a great nation." Then God opened her eyes and she saw a well of water. So she went and filled the skin with water and gave the boy a drink. (Genesis 21:17-19)

God now gives Hagar His *peace* in the place of her fear (v. 17). He provides a *personal promise*. He grants to her a new *future*, a new *purpose* for life (v. 18). God demonstrates that He will be her *provider*, miraculously when necessary (v. 19).

Many of us have secondhand relationships with God. We have sung everyone else's hymns. We have echoed the reverent prayers and praises of others. We have hitchhiked on everyone else's faith. We have lived on our religious heritage. Tragically, these are all empty and bankrupt experiences if they have not led to a firsthand, intimate relationship with Christ.

At the end of ourselves God's Word will begin to speak to us personally.

Our problem is that we don't realize how desperately we need God. We have all we need and want; we are satisfied with our lives. So God pursues us to bring us to our senses spiritually, to reduce us to the heights of knowing Him personally and intimately.

EXPERIENCING GOD

As it was with Hagar, at the end of ourselves God's Word will begin to speak to us personally. Passages that were often nice but remote will anchor themselves in our hearts with a deep sense of significance. We can expect God's promises to become personal realities to which we cling in the swift torrent of trouble. When difficulties have demolished our dreams, God gives us a new dream—His dream for us. You can expect God to provide, perhaps dramatically. There *will* be a well in the wilderness; an ending in which all things have worked together for good. In it all, you will come to know the Lord as *your* God. As Hagar said in her first encounter with God, "You are the God who sees *me* (Genesis 16:13; italics added).

Gideon needed to know and demonstrate the sufficiency of God. When he came against the Midianites, God instituted a troop "build down" proposal. The army was reduced to three hundred men. Why? So that Israel would not falsely boast in her own power (Judges 7:2). The Israelites needed to know the power of God firsthand, that God alone is sufficient. All God needed at Midian was three hundred witnesses.

David came against Goliath as a young man. Saul offered David the sufficiency of his armor (1 Samuel 17:38-39). Saul was large; he stood head and shoulders above everyone else (9:2). In Saul's armor David would have taken two steps before the armor moved. Saul's sufficiency would have got in David's way.

David knew the sufficiency of God. He said to Saul, "The Lord who delivered me from the paw of the lion and the paw of the bear will deliver me from the hand of this Philistine" (17:37). David refused to walk around in anyone else's armor and was personally victorious in the sufficiency of God.

---

*When God uses pain to bring us
to the end of ourselves,
He will meet us there.*

There were times in the early part of our ministry when our income fell short of our expenses, times when there was too much month left at the end of the money. That was difficult for us. It was troubling to see others who were prospering. It was a struggle to park our old, beat-up car next to shiny up-to-date models.

But God was in it all. At the beginning of our married life and ministry, God wanted to teach me and my wife something central to our faith: His sufficiency to meet all our needs. So He stripped away our sufficiency and faithfully, miraculously at times, met *every* single need. He clothed us. He supplied for us. He personally cared for us. I wouldn't trade what we learned as a family about our God for anything. But God had to reduce my ability to make money to show us His love and power.

Debbie Jackson Searles was a student and a part of that first church we pastored. She was a happy, helpful person. Friends often came to her for counsel and encouragement. Then, surprisingly, Deb went through a crisis that left her severely depressed. Unable to climb out of it, she was ultimately hospitalized. In time, the doctors diagnosed a problem with her body chemistry and, with proper medication, they were able to restore her to her original vitality.

She told me later that God had tailor-made that trauma for her. As she said, "I was not living in any 'big' sin, but God needed to purge out a growing sense of pride and self-sufficiency. I needed to be aware of His presence and place in my life."

Deb left that crisis with a new song in her heart. I'll never forget hearing Christine Wyrtzen sing the song that Debbie wrote. I listened. The words pierced my heart:

> I've been through a fire
>   That has deepened my desire
> To know the living God more and more.
>   It hasn't been much fun,
> But the work that it has done
>   In my life has made it worth the hurt.
> You see, sometimes we need the hard times
>   To bring us to our knees,
> Otherwise we do as we please and never heed Him.
>   But He always knows what's best,
> And it's when we are distressed
>   That we really come to know God as He is.

Don was a top executive in the prime of his career. A heart attack and an ensuing stroke left him unable to remember basic everyday things. But Don came through this crisis with a new and fresh touch of the Lord. He talked more about how much he loved the Lord, how he had finally sensed God's personal reality in his life. Don took the initiative to pray with his wife about things that they never prayed about before. He became more sensitive to his family with a new warmth and tenderness. God cracked Don's shell and began a significant work in his life. When Don's own significance was gone, things of true significance came to the fore.

It's no wonder that the psalmist declares:

> Whom have I in heaven but you?
> And earth has nothing I desire besides you.
> My flesh and my heart may fail,
> but God is the strength of my heart
> and my portion forever.
> (Psalm 73:25-26)

BLOOM WHERE YOU ARE PLANTED

Often, when crisis reduces our sufficiency, a new life situation will emerge. It was that way for Hagar. She could not return to Abraham and Sarah. Ishmael would marry. Hagar would begin a new life. She bloomed where she was planted.

Don't look back. Don't long for past comfort and security. God knows that if we go back, we may become self-sufficient again. Be productive in God's place for you.

When God uses pain to bring us to the end of ourselves, He will meet us there. He will be there with His Word for you, His certain promises, His provisions.

God knows that the only sufficiency that is truly sufficient in life is the sufficiency of Himself. So He works until He has us singing:

I need Thee every hour,
In joy or pain;
Come quickly and abide
Or life is vain.

I need Thee, O I need Thee;
Every hour I need Thee;
O bless me now, my Savior,
I come to Thee!
(Annie S. Hawks)

10

Platforming His Power

The Strategic Issues of
Credibility and Visibility

A lot of people know where they are going and how they are going to get there. Take, for example, the materialist. He lives to accumulate. The hedonist lives for pleasure and knows right where to go to get it. The self-fulfiller lives for the big number one. Each of those persons has a well-defined sense of purpose.

Unfortunately, many believers either adopt the purposes of the world or have no idea what their purpose in life should be. Some have purposes that vacillate, depending on who they are with or what they have recently read. Their life flows like a meandering stream. They have no voice for themselves. They are like an echo.

Thankfully, God wants to help us establish a purpose for our lives. God's purpose for us is that we *glorify* Him. It is the reason for our redemption (1 Corinthians 6:19-20; Romans 8:29-30). It is the all-consuming focus of our existence and the measure of our maturity (1 Corinthians 10:31; 2 Corinthians 3:18).

Basically, glorifying God means reflecting His nature. Glorifying God means being image-bearers who mirror the love, mercy, power, righteousness, justice, and other aspects of God. It means giving *visibility* to His invisibility, *credibility* to His existence.

Difficulty in our lives attracts the attention of others.

God's glory is the essence of His very being. He knows that the ultimate health and welfare of the human race depends on our knowing Him. God is made known through those of us who are His children. It is our privileged assignment to reveal Him before a watching world.

God uses several means to reveal His glory. The sun, stars, and moon reveal His power and creativity. Israel revealed what God was like as He opened the sea for them and defeated armies far beyond their ability. Christ was God's glory in the flesh. The Bible reveals the glory of God. And you and I are added to the list. That puts us in significant company. It is a high and privileged responsibility. It is our purpose in living to provide both credibility and visibility to God.

DIFFICULTY: A PRELUDE TO GOD'S GLORY

Difficulty in our lives attracts the attention of others. People around stop to notice. They talk to you, talk to others about you, do things to help you, and periodically ask to see how you are doing. Seemingly unnoticed, even uninteresting people draw a crowd when they go through difficulty. Trouble is often God's way of saying to the world around us, "May I have your attention, please?"

So it was with a man who had been blind from birth (John 9:1). He was well-known for his begging on the Temple steps. As he begged day by day, he gained high visibility. His trouble had placed him in the lime-light. If God is to be visible, then He must catch the attention and interest of a fast-moving, earthly-minded world.

Not only had the blind man captured the people's attention, but he had also *aroused their curiosity.* The disciples asked Christ, "Rabbi, who sinned, this man or his parents, that he was born blind?" (9:2) The rabbis of Christ's day thought that the consequences of the parents' sins would be reaped in the children of the sinning parents. Since this man was born blind, could it have been because of his parents? Or did he sin in his mother's womb? As we have discussed, the curious controversy reflects the then prevalent position that the only purpose in pain was punishment for sin.

Pain is a setting in which we can uniquely magnify God.

In the midst of their curiosity, Christ deepened their perspectives on pain by telling them there was another purpose, a greater, nobler purpose.

Parenthetically, Christ provides here a great lesson in how we need to respond to others as He steps above the controversy with a commitment to *compassion.* He cares about the blind man's eyes. The disciples, by contrast, are more interested in the theology of the trouble than the trauma of the trouble. They are more curious than compassionate. They had seen Christ do many miracles. It would have been an act of compassion for them to have pointed out the man born blind to Christ and asked Him to heal him. Then, after the need was met, they could have inquired of the reason for his pain.

We are prone to the same malady. It is more comfortable to be curious about another's pain than it is to be compassionate and constructive. We often spend more time talking about people's problems than we spend reaching out to them. We spend more time wondering *why* than we do praying.

Compassion must always rise above the curiosity. Healing needs to be our priority as we look toward those who hurt. It is not that we should be uninterested in truth and knowledge; it's that things need to be put in their proper place. Christ here demonstrates that God turns a compassionate face toward those who struggle. We, too, must look to people who hurt with a caring heart and not just a curious eye.

Christ's compassion is the beginning of the unfolding of God's purpose in this man's pain. Christ explains that the man was born blind to give *credibility* and *visibility* to God. "Neither this man nor his parents sinned, . . . but this happened so that the work of God might be displayed in his life" (9:3).

John selects this story to support the credibility of Christ's claims as God and the true Savior of mankind (20:30-31). John consistently uses the word *work* to indicate a miracle that affirms the credibility of Christ's link to the Father and His claims as the Messiah. Christ claimed that He was sent from the Father (9:4). This miracle would give credibility to that claim. Christ also claimed that He was the "light" of the world (v. 5). This miracle would beautifully demonstrate that claim by taking the man from darkness to light.

The man was born blind to provide visibility for God, "so that the work of God might be displayed" (9:3). The word *displayed* literally means to reveal, to make known. God has chosen not to keep Himself a secret. Through this man's trouble, God is going to make

Himself known. The invisible God will become visible. We will see the Father's compassion and power.

As Christ said, all of this would happen "in his life," that is, in the life of the man born blind. We are the channel, the stage for God's glory. Our difficulty and pain come into perspective when we see them in the light of the high privilege of giving the claims of Christ credibility and the power of God visibility.

The second key to cooperating with God's plan is to give witness.

It may be that the claim that God's "grace is sufficient" will become credible. In trouble, we can reflect God by making visible His patience and His forgiveness. We can exhibit God's willingness to suffer so that others can be helped. It may very well be that a miraculous healing will give visibility to God's power.

Recently, a woman in our church went through a terribly difficult period. Her unsaved parents were overwhelmed with not only the stability that came with her confidence in Christ, but also with the tremendous outpouring of care and concern shown by her Christian friends. The trouble caught their attention and, as they were watching, God was glorified.

Pain is a setting in which we can uniquely magnify God.

GOD'S GLORY AMONG THE MASSES

Having said this, [Jesus] spit on the ground, made some mud with the saliva, and put it on the man's eyes. "Go," he told him, "wash in the pool of Siloam." ... So the man went and washed, and came home seeing. (John 9:6-7)

What can we expect as we glorify God through our pain? The responses of those in John 9 help us to know the kind of reception God's glory will receive around us.

First, some will see and *seek*. When his neighbors and friends saw the healed man, they couldn't believe it was the same man who had been blind. He said, "I am the man" (9:9). Then he told them of Christ. His testimony made Christ credible and visible. They asked anxiously, "Where is this man?" (v. 12) The works of God had cut a path of preevangelism through the blind man's neighborhood. They sought to find Christ and know more about Him.

Why did a pagan harlot from Jericho come to believe in the God of Israel? Because God glorified Himself through Israel when He dried up the Red Sea. He demonstrated His credibility and visibility when Israel defeated the mighty armies of the Amorites. The word spread—all the way to Jericho and into Rahab's heart. God's glory through Israel cut a path of preevangelism in her heart (Joshua 2:8-11).

A couple in my first ministry took the time and made the effort to put their difficult marriage together on God's terms. It caught the attention of their neighbors. Seeing God glorified in their home, a couple in the neighborhood began to seek God. They came and asked why. They heard about Jesus Christ and soon received Him as Savior.

Others, however, will see God's works and remain *silent*. The blind man's parents were intimidated by the Pharisees. They feared they would be excommunicated from the synagogue (John 9:18-22). Many fear the price of claiming Christ as Savior. What will He demand? What will they lose in gaining Him? So they silently watch. They take notes in their hearts. That's good. God will work quietly in their silence to capitalize on what they have seen.

Then there are those who will be *set against* what they see. No one knew more about this event than the Pharisees. They interviewed the blind man twice (9:13-16, 24-34) and his parents once (vv. 18-23). Yet the Pharisees refused to accept the clear evidence. Some are so set against God that they refuse to seek Him regardless of the evidence. Think of what they did to Christ, who was a walking catalog of evidence. In the face of the dramatic display of God's credibility and visibility through Christ, they crucified Him. We should never assume that all people will come to Christ when they see Him magnified in our trouble.

OBEDIENT WITNESS

One key question remains. If God should choose my life and my pain as a platform for His glory, how can I cooperate? How can I be sure that His purpose will come to pass?

Two things in the blind man's response are key to his privileged place in God's plan. First, in his trouble he *obeyed the Master* (John 9:6-7). Christ put mud on his eyes and told him to wash in the pool of Siloam. "So the man went and washed, and came home seeing" (v. 7). The revelation of God's glory depended on the man's obedience to Christ's commands. So it is with us. Our unconditional surrender to all that Christ tells us to do sets the stage for His glory.

If my pain is from the injury of another's careless actions against me, then I hear Christ say, "Forgive them." That's the pool in which I wash my eyes. When money fails, Christ says, "Seek ye first the kingdom of God, and his righteousness; and all these things shall be added unto you" (Matthew 6:33, KJV). Therefore, biblical stewardship remains intact for Christ's kingdom; we don't abandon righteousness to make a little extra money. We don't forsake family responsibilities. We stay in

the path of righteousness so that God's power and glory
are revealed. We refuse to become bitter. We trust God
to deal with our enemies and love them in return. We
refuse to extend anger. We refuse to stop reaching out
with a servant's heart. We wash in the pool of His will
and gladly obey.

The second key to cooperating with God's plan is
to give *witness*. The blind man happily gave credit to
Christ before his neighbors, his parents, and the hostile
Jewish leaders. He did it with tact and with courage. He
did it even when it meant dismissal from the Temple
(John 9:34).

As God works in our life, we must tactfully pro-
claim His glory. Give credit where credit is due. If God
delivers us through prayer, then let it be known that
God answers prayer. If God provides sustaining grace,
then let it be known that we are making it because His
mighty hand is supporting you. Christ opened the blind
man's eyes to bring glory to His Father. Nobody in our
world will know the credibility and visibility of God if
we lock them up as hidden secrets in the closet of our
lives.

When the psalmist asked God to help him, he
prayed, "May God be gracious to us and bless us and
make his face shine upon us" (Psalm 67:1). Why? That
God's ways "may be known on earth, [and His] salvation among all nations" (v. 2).

If God heals, helps, holds, or delivers, we must let
our world know.

Their wedding was scheduled for August. Several
months before, cancer was discovered in one lung of the
bride-to-be. They postponed, and she began her treat-
ments. Many prayed—specifically and intensely. After
her first treatment, the doctors were amazed. They
could find no trace of the cancer.

At Christmas, the bride and groom were united in marriage. They made clear to me that they wanted all at the wedding to know what God had done. It was my joy.

A woman in our church came to me and said, "Pastor, I have a confession to make." She then told me how several weeks earlier, her husband had written a check for God's work through their local church. This couple's business had been slow, and they were financially to the wall. She told him they couldn't afford to do it. He replied, "We can't afford *not* to do it." So they did. She said that since they took that step of obedience, God had blessed them beyond their dreams. Their business had increased fourfold. "I learned a great lesson, Pastor, about the faithfulness of God. I wish I could tell everyone. In fact," she continued, "you have my permission to tell anyone you wish."

We have a purpose, a divine destiny. Our purpose is to glorify God through our lives. If God should select you to bring glory to Him in this world through pain, do it well. Obey. Bear witness. Through your suffering, some may seek and find the Savior. Let them hear you sing:

> To God be the glory,
> Great things He hath done!

11

Job's Unusual Task
"Thou Art Worthy"

Why?
Why me? Why now? Why again? Why don't You
help me? Why God, why?

Trouble persistently taunts us with its questions.
Yet God does supply us with answers. He teaches us
that pain exists because of the problem of sin. We know
that pain can be used to conform us to Christ's image,
that pain can pay off in power. It is pain that draws us
from disobedience to obedience. We may experience
the painful tearing away of the layers of our sufficiency
to help us become God-sufficient. God may permit pain
to reduce the risk in our lives. God may even use pain to
make us usable for Him or to demonstrate His power
and glory on the earth.

But what do you do when all the answers to pain
elude you? When you shout, *"Why?"* and there is a
great silence. When from your perspective, the suffering makes absolutely no sense at all.

So it was for Job. Job suffered intensely over a long
period of time. Though Job never knew why, there was

a reason for his pain. With God, there is *always* a reason. He never permits pain without a purpose. We have the distinct advantage of knowing that purpose.

Job's Suffering Was a Showcase

> In the land of Uz there lived a man whose name was Job. This man was blameless and upright; he feared God and shunned evil. He had seven sons and three daughters, and he owned seven thousand sheep, three thousand camels, five hundred yoke of oxen and five hundred donkeys, and had a large number of servants. He was the greatest man among all the people of the East. (Job 1:1-3)

The stage is set in the verses that follow this description of Job (vv. 6-12).

Knowing what we do, I feel like shouting, "Job, don't flinch. . . . You can't imagine how important this is."

In essence, Satan said to God, "Job is righteous and worships You because You are good to him. You have made him rich and You have not permitted any evil to befall him. If You took all this away, he would curse You to Your face."

Can you grasp what Satan has just said? He has said that God is not worthy of a man's worship and loyalty in and of Himself. Instead, God has to buy our love. Men do not value God for who He is, but only for what He does for them. The glory of God has been slandered in front of the heavenly host. It's as though all the eyes of the universe turn questioningly toward God. Is God worthy of a man's loyalty, worship, and praise regardless? What kind of God is He anyway?

We go to great lengths to protect our reputations from slander. By comparison, our reputations aren't worth being concerned about. General Ariel Sharon traveled to New York to file a $50 million lawsuit against *Time* magazine, which had accused him of complicity in a massacre in Beirut, Lebanon. He had to clear his name. General William Westmoreland took CBS to court in a multimillion dollar lawsuit to protect himself against their supposed slandering of his handling of the View Nam War.

How much more should God's name be upheld. God could not simply ignore Satan's charge; it was far too serious.

Who would come to God's defense? Job. Job was called upon to prove a point on God's behalf. He would suffer to prove the worthiness of God. There could be no higher calling. God, as the sentinel at the gate of Job's life, opened the gate, and Job's troubles began at the hand of Satan.

Knowing what we do, I feel like shouting, "Job, don't flinch. Make it through. You can't imagine how important this is." I cheer as Job finishes the first act in this tragic drama. He has lost everything, including his sons and daughters (Job 1:13-19). Yet, he closes Act I in grief and agony, still worshiping his God:

> At this, Job got up and tore his robe and shaved his head. Then he fell to the ground in worship and said:

> "Naked I came from my mother's womb,
>   and naked I will depart.
> The Lord gave and the Lord has taken away;
>   may the name of the Lord be praised."

> In all this, Job did not sin by charging God with wrongdoing. (Vv. 20-22)

Job proved the worthiness of God to be praised regardless.

Satan was persistent. He slandered God again by saying that the problem is that God had not permitted him to touch Job's body (2:1-5). Satan assumed that Job will fold and curse God if his health and comfort were at stake. Satan will stop at nothing. He is willing to waste anything and anybody to get to God's glory. God trusted Job with the challenge and prohibited Satan from taking Job's life.

> So Satan went out from the presence of the Lord and afflicted Job with painful sores from the soles of his feet to the top of his head. Then Job took a piece of broken pottery and scraped himself with it as he sat among the ashes. (Vv. 7-8)

Job's wife entered the scene at that point and comforted Job with some sage advice: "Curse God and die!" (v. 9) That's just what Satan wanted Job to do. That would play right into his hands. My spirit shouts to Job as he plays out the scene: "Don't do it, Job. Don't give up."

Some of our trouble may be the result of an invisible conflict taking place in the spiritual realm.

Then Job spoke. In the midst of the ashes, he affirmed, "'You are talking like a foolish woman. Shall we accept good from God, and not trouble?' In all this, Job did not sin in what he said" (v. 10).

Job has done it. God's name has been magnified in the midst of his misery. And all the time, Job had no way of knowing why. Yet Job was loyal to God above his possessions and beyond his personal comfort. God is indeed a worthy God.

On the stage of our own lives Satan duplicates the scene. God's Word calls him the "accuser of our brothers, who accuses them before our God day and night" (Revelation 12:10).

It is a high calling to prove the worthiness of God in the face of Satan's accusations. Whether in pain or pleasure, we can constantly prove with our lives that God is worthy above all else in life. That was Job's privilege. Even though he had done it in the face of intense trouble and wrenching pain.

There were other reasons for Job's suffering. God knew that *we* needed a demonstration that true faith in God is more than a self-serving faith. Satan kicked the props out from under Job, and Job proved that his faith was anchored in that which is far greater—his God. Some religionists will tell you that if you have enough faith, you can be happy, healthy, and wealthy. Faith to them is a way to *get* good things from God. Job lost it all. Yet he remained a man of faith.

Faith is our unshakable belief in God, His Word, and His character. True faith stands above and beyond the trouble and triumphs of life. When life demolished Job, it did not demolish his faith. If trouble demolishes our faith, it is a reflection that our faith was only a faith for protection, peace, and pleasure. A shallow, selfish faith.

Job's suffering also proves that some of our trouble may be the result of an invisible conflict taking place in the spiritual realm. Struggles that have meaning beyond my job, my roommate, my family, or my peace. Ephesians 6 clearly speaks to the issue of a whole network of Satan's forces battling against God and against His people. Paul writes, "For our struggle is not against flesh and blood, but against the rulers, against the authorities, against the powers of this dark world and against the spiritual forces of evil in the heavenly realms" (Ephesians 6:12).

It is important for us to know that some of the "whys" in our lives have answers in another realm. Sometimes we struggle with pain to prove ultimate universal principles before the throne of God. Not all of suffering has an answer on earth but may well be a part of a conflict in another sphere. A sphere in which our faithfulness generates a victory on behalf of God.

Last, Job's suffering helps to chart a course for us. Job shows us a way to suffer well. He demonstrates that we don't need to have all our questions answered to survive. Job had *no* answers. He had no idea of what was happening beyond the reaches of this earth. All he had was God and a faith that refused to quit. A belief that in spite of all that was happening around him, God was still God and as such deserved his unflinching allegiance. Job charted the course through the waters of seemingly senseless trouble. As a pacesetter for us, Job demonstrates success in suffering in two ways. First, we can all identify with him in that he suffered severely. Second, Job made it through this severe struggle because he knew and trusted God.

JOB SUFFERED SEVERELY

When we hurt we are often encouraged to turn to Christ who suffered for us, leaving an example for us to follow. And well we should. But we are tempted to think that He had a divine edge. Job was *only* human. That doesn't discount Christ's help in our need; it simply provides Job as an example of a mortal who made it. Notice the breadth of Job's suffering.

Job suffered the loss of all his *external worth*—children, houses, livestock, riches. Even Job's wife was disgusted with him. He lost it *all.* His world became a heap of ashes. Many of us base our worth and self-esteem on externals. We shouldn't, but we often do. It's where we live, what we drive, who we know, the size of our bank account, or the title on the door of our corporate office that establishes our worth and sense of self-esteem. But God calls us to base our esteem and worth in our relationship with Him. As we internalize our relationship with God, we develop true self-esteem and true worth. That's where Job was. Even though Job was the the most righteous and the richest man of his day, when everything was demolished around him, *he* was not demolished. He still had his God and his God had him.

What he needed from his friends was grace, *not guilt.*

Job's suffering was also *physical, mental,* and *emotional* (2:2). His body began to disintegrate; he was racked with pain. Job went through great seasons of depression and mental confusion, which were complicated by the advice of his friends.

Job was subjected to the *bad counsel of good friends.* It began with Job's wife. Let's not be too hard on her. Have you ever watched a loved one suffer? You know how quickly it gets to you. In despair, she counseled him, "Curse God and die!" (2:9) Yet Job found the strength to resist the temptations of his wife's words.

Then there were the three friends who came and gave advice: "Job, you have sinned. That's why this happened to you. Repent and recover."

Nine times they repeated their charge. Nine times Job responded, "It's not true." Back and forth they go, wearing one another down.

Even well-meaning friends tend to complicate our trouble. They mean their words to be like salve, but instead they are like swords. These friends are like those modern-day prophets who tell us that *all* trouble, sickness, and sorrow come from unconfessed sin in our lives. May God shield us from this kind of destructive advice. It was not true of Job. He suffered for a more noble cause. What he needed from his friends was *grace*, not guilt. At the end of Job's suffering, God called the three friends before Him and reproved them for their bad counsel and called on them to repent (42:7-9).

Job's suffering was severe because of the *memories* (29:2-25). When we lose, we are left only with the memories. Difficulty often leaves us without the things we used to possess. Without people who were precious to us. Without a husband. Without a wife. Without good health. Without fame. Without income. Then the memories of all that used to be haunt our spirits. The memories of what we had and lost. They are memories that only serve to magnify our misery.

Affirming God's sovereignty in life, death, wisdom, and power, Job was able to say, "God, I trust You."

Job's suffering was also severe because he had *no support*. Where was his pastor? Who was his psychiatrist? What medication could he take? Job had no books to read on grief and pain. He didn't even have a "significant loss seminar" that he could attend. No family. Friends were a problem. He couldn't even read the Bible. Yet Job made it. He and God alone.

In all of this, Satan has reduced Job to the irreducible minimum—Job and his God. That's right where Satan wants him. Now, Job, all you have is God. Will you curse Him or praise His name?

Job is indeed a pacesetter. Under *severe difficulty* he refuses to depart from loyally worshiping his God. And in all of it, he didn't know why. How did he do it?

JOB KNEW HIS GOD

The theme of the book of Job is not patience, though we learn something of patience from Job's life (James 5:10-11). The theme is not Job and Satan. It is not even Satan and God. The theme of this book is not suffering.

The theme of the book of Job is God. Who is God? And is He worthy of man's unconditional, uncompromised allegiance? Does God have the right to exercise His sovereignty? These are the issues of the book. Does God have the right to call the shots in our lives even when we don't understand? When it makes no sense, Job answers, "Yes!" *YES!* A thousand times, yes. Yes, in spite of everything.

What did Job know about God that enabled him in trouble?

Job knew that God had the right to be *sovereign in life* (Job 1:21). God permitted Job's life to turn upside down. "The Lord gave, and the Lord hath taken away; blessed be the name of the Lord" (v. 21; KJV). We don't love God for what He does for us in life; we love Him because He is the God of our life. The day after Christ fed the five thousand, the same people showed up for another spectacular meal. Christ refused. Many left Him that day. They were in it for the "goodies." When Christ told His followers that they would be persecuted for His sake, Scripture says that many left Him (John 6:53-66).

On the poverty-stricken island of Haiti, children follow you down the street begging for money. If you give them some, they keep following you. If you refuse, they scorn you and walk away. How tragic that some of us treat God that way.

God is the sovereign over all of life. A friend of mine officiated at the burial of a baby. As the mourners walked up the hillside to the grave site, the minister admitted that he really didn't know what to say. The mother of the child, with tears on her cheeks, said quietly, "The Lord gives and the Lord takes away. Blessed be the name of the Lord."

Job also knew that God was *sovereign in death*. In the face of death, Job said, "Though he slay me, yet will I hope in him" (Job 13:15). It is as though Job says, "Lord, even if You take my life, I will still affirm my trust in You. Nothing, not even death will sever my loyal allegiance to Your name." (Compare Philippians 1:19-24.)

Job knew that God was *sovereign in wisdom and in power*. Near the end of his testing, Job teeters in his confusion and pain. God meets him and stabilizes his failing heart by reminding Job of His infinite, unchallenged wisdom and power (chaps. 38-41). God asks, "Were you there when I created the heavens and the earth? Did you ever see their cornerstone? Where are their foundations laid?" On and on, question after question. God is driving home His point. He is so vastly superior to us in wisdom and power that anything less than submission to His plan for our lives would be foolish. In all that God does, though it may be painful, though it may escape our understanding, yet He is wise. Always wise.

Affirming God's sovereignty in life, death, wisdom, and power, Job was able to say, "God, I trust You." That's how Job made it. And through it all, he proved the point. He shamed Satan and glorified the matchless name of God.

I love him for it.

He is my hero.

Job realized that in suffering the issue is not *why*. The issue is *who*. That, too, is the issue for us. We rest in the reality that our God is the true and the living God, worthy of our trust regardless. We affirm that He has the right to be the sovereign God of life and death, the sovereign God of wisdom and power. Though this may not make the hurt any less painful, it *does* get us through victoriously in a way that honors Him.

Since God always knows what He is doing, all we have to know is Him. When the whys swarm around us, when our question marks go unanswered, when all the answers seem so shallow—get beyond them to the who. You can trust God. He'll see you through.

> Oh, the depth of the riches of
> the wisdom and knowledge of God!
> How unsearchable his judgments,
> and his paths beyond tracing out!
> "Who has known the mind of the Lord?
> Or who has been his counselor?"
> "Who has ever given to God,
> that God should repay him?"
> For from him and through him
> and to him are all things.
> To him be the glory forever!
> Amen.
> (Romans 11:33-36)

12

Why Do the Wicked Prosper?
Seeing All the Way to Eternity

There is a flip side to the issue of believers who struggle. It is, "Why do I struggle when wicked people seem to be so free of trouble?"

We should not be surprised when the righteous suffer. It conforms us to the image of Christ. It gives us power in witness. It instills the valuable strength of God-sufficiency and reduces the risk in our ministry for God. It refines us to make us capable and usable. It catches the attention of a watching world so that God's glory may be seen as He becomes credible and visible through our suffering. It may even be used in a sphere far beyond ourselves to glorify God in the universe.

Don't pity the righteous who suffer. They have a divine edge. Their resource in pain is the reality that God is there and they only experience what He permits. And all that He permits is guaranteed by the kind of God He is. The righteous suffer with the knowledge that Christ has conquered and gives grace, growth, and glory in the midst of pain.

The question that plagues me is not so much why do the righteous suffer, but why do the wicked prosper? Why is it that my competitor in business can cheat his customers and strike unethical deals and drive a new Cadillac, while in my commitment to righteousness I have to drive a beat-up old car? Why does my neighbor, who goes fishing every Sunday morning while I'm at church, catch the biggest and best fish when I can hardly catch a thing on Monday? Why are the ungodly those who belong to the jet set? Why should my neighbor, who has been cheating on his wife for years, have such nice children while mine are driving me crazy? Why is it so hard and challenging to walk the Christian walk when unsaved people seem to have no restraints at all?

If all we see is the world around us, then we will surely fall.

INSTABILITY

The psalmist struggled with this as well. In fact, it created a tremendous instability and vulnerability in his life. "As for me, my feet had almost slipped; I had nearly lost my foothold. For I envied the arrogant when I saw the prosperity of the wicked" (Psalm 73:2-3).

Envying the wicked puts us in a precarious place. It is dangerous to our spiritual health. Think of how many of God's people have compromised themselves to try to keep up with the pagan world. It is a great temptation to worship at the temple of prosperity. It is easy to begin to suspect that righteousness is less than rewarding, a divine deterrent to wealth and gain.

If all we see is the world around us, then we will surely fall. The psalmist looked around him and felt absolutely cheated when he compared his life to the prosperity of the pagans. In his misery, he relates every detail of their gain. People who are in the clutches of misery always can give detailed accounts of their problems. Over and over again we rehearse our reasons for feeling so bad. In the process, our problems often become somewhat exaggerated. So it was with Asaph, the author of Psalm 73.

> For I envied the arrogant
> when I saw the prosperity of the wicked.
>
> They have no struggles;
> their bodies are healthy and strong.
> They are free from the burdens common to man;
> they are not plagued by human ills.
> Therefore pride is their necklace;
> they clothe themselves with violence.
> From their callous hearts comes iniquity;
> the evil conceits of their minds know no limits.
> They scoff and speak with malice;
> in their arrogance they threaten oppression.
> Their mouths lay claim to heaven,
> and their tongues take possession of the earth.
> Therefore their people turn to them
> and drink up waters in abundance.
> They say, "How can God know?
> Does the Most High have knowledge?"
>
> This is what the wicked are like—
> always carefree, they increase in wealth.
>
> (Psalm 73:3-12)

SELF-PITY

At this point, Asaph throws himself a pity party. In his pity, he bemoans the fact that his commitment to personal purity has netted him nothing (Psalm 73:13). A slight exaggeration—but when you are into self-pity, it's hard to be positive.

> Surely in vain have I kept my heart pure;
>   in vain have I washed my hands in innocence.
> All day long I have been plagued;
>   I have been punished every morning.
>
> If I had said, "I will speak thus,"
>   I would have betrayed this generation of your
>   children.
> When I tried to understand all this,
>   it was oppressive to me.
>
> (Psalm 73:13-16)

Asaph is obviously more interested in cash than in character. He wants his righteousness to pay off in dollars and cents, in physical strength rather than in spiritual health. He wants his God to function like a heavenly Santa Claus. And since He hasn't, Asaph is discouraged and ready to drop out. He is walking around defeated and pretending that everything is OK (v. 15).

---

*If all you see is the here and now,
you will misunderstand everything.*

Had I been alive in Naboth's day I would have struggled with the issue of pagan prosperity. Naboth was a common Israelite who owned a portion of land on which he had planted a vineyard. King Ahab wanted Naboth's land for an herb garden. He invited Naboth to deal with him, and Naboth refused. That was his family's land. It was Naboth's heritage. In that day, inherited land was a family treasure to be passed on for generations. No price could buy it from Naboth. Naboth was a man of true values.

Ahab, the unjust king of Israel, pouted in his bedroom. Jezebel, his wife, asked him what was wrong. He told her about Naboth's field and how he couldn't have it for his herb garden. How sad.

Well, Jezebel would see to it that Ahab got his garden. She hired two false witnesses who testified that Naboth had cursed God and the king. They took Naboth outside the city and stoned him to death. Ahab had his herb garden (1 Kings 21:1-16).

Though God ultimately dealt with Ahab and Jezebel, at this point my heart cries out, *Where is God? Why do the wicked prosper?*

GOD'S BIG PICTURE

This text teaches us that in the scope of eternity, the wicked do not prosper. Just in the nick of time, Asaph looked to God for his answer. "It was oppressive to me till I entered the sanctuary of God; then I understood *their final destiny*" (Psalm 73:16-17; italics added).

Destiny. Life is far more than the here and now. Life spans the years on into eternity. When the psalmist looked to God, his perspective changed drastically. He ceased envying the wicked and found spiritual stability again.

I have a friend who says that if all you see is the here and now, you will misunderstand everything. How true. We must reject the two-dimensional focus of the here and now and let the third dimension of God's perspective always dictate our perceptions.

As a child, I enjoyed "3-D" comic books. A special set of cardboard glasses came with the comic books. Without the glasses, the books were blurred and unclear. With the glasses, they became distinct and alive with action and color. Seeing life through God's glasses will always clarify and provide an accurate assessment of life around us.

From God's point of view, the wicked are not in an enviable position. As the psalmist says, "Surely you place them on slippery ground; you cast them down to ruin.

How suddenly are they destroyed, completely swept away by terrors! As a dream when one awakes, so when you arise, O Lord, you will despise them as fantasies" (Psalm 73:18-20).

Is it a sign of prosperity to stand before God and hear Him say, "Depart from Me, you who are cursed, into the eternal fire prepared for the devil and his angels" (Matthew 25:41)? As Christ said, "What good will it be for a man if he gains the whole world, yet forfeits his soul?" (16:26)

In Luke 12 Christ tells of a wealthy man who was so prosperous that he had to tear down his old barns and build new ones. He anticipated being able to say to himself, "'You have plenty of good things laid up for many years. Take life easy; eat, drink and be merry.' But God said to him, 'You fool! This very night your life will be demanded from you. Then who will get what you have prepared for yourself?'" (Luke 12: 19-20) Christ concluded by saying, "This is how it will be with anyone who stores up things for himself but is not rich toward God" (Luke 12:21).

> *The prosperity of the wicked will quiet the objection of some who [say], "If You had been good to me . . . I would have believed in You."*

SAND CASTLES

Our family often vacations in Florida. We love the sand and the ocean. When we arrive, my plans are to hit the beach and relax. My children's plans are to play in the water and build sand castles. They usually succeed in dragging me to the water's edge, where plans for a phenomenal sand castle are begun. I reluctantly begin to help (strictly parental duty), but soon find myself excitedly absorbed in the project. In fact, about halfway through, the kids are off somewhere else as I am designing and building the most spectacular sand castle on the beach. Seaweed forms ivy on the walls. Towers are topped with flags. Weeds from the dunes make palm trees for the landscape. People stop and inquire. Some say, "Who built that?" I nod proudly. Then it's time to go home. I leave the labor of my hands, the product of my own creativity. The next day we return. My sand castle is gone, washed out to sea. The tide has done me in.

So it is with the fleeting nature of earthly prosperity in the tide of God's judgment. What good is it if you have one big inning, yet lose the whole game? From God's point of view, the wicked are not in an enviable position.

Yet why should they prosper even now? I am convinced it is designed as living proof of God's mercy and grace. What a picture of God's willingness to withhold judgment and give them what they don't deserve. The prosperity of the wicked is a divine reminder of God's mercy and grace. As we see the wicked prosper, our own hearts should overflow with praise because we too are recipients of that mercy and grace.

Not only is the prosperity of the wicked proof of God's mercy and grace, but it is also proof of the perversity of human hearts. God's overflowing goodness tends to drive the masses to greater independence, rebellion, and wickedness. The prosperity of the wicked will quiet the objection of some who will want to excuse themselves from judgment by saying, "If You had been good to me, if You had made me prosperous, I would have believed in You!" Not so. Mankind's heart is "deceitful above all things" (Jeremiah 17:9).

TRUE PROSPERITY

Asaph comes before God embarrassed for envying the wicked. He admits to his shame: "I was senseless and ignorant; I was a brute beast before you" (Psalm 73:22).

Then Asaph redefines prosperity. He affirms that in God he has *true prosperity.* That is why he began his psalm with the joyful acclamation "Surely God is good to Israel, to those who are pure in heart" (v. 1).

Asaph is prosperous because of *God's continued presence* with him (v. 23). As the writer of Hebrews says, "Keep your lives free from the love of money and be content with what you have, because God has said, 'Never will I leave you: never will I forsake you'" (Hebrews 13:5). If God is with us, we have all we will ever need.

Asaph prospers because of *God's protection.* "You hold me by my right hand" (Psalm 73:23). He prospers in the fact that *God guides him* (v. 24). Those apart from God do not have the prosperity of His guidance. The best they can do is experiment in the darkness. Ultimately, God's people prosper in the ultimate reward of their faith. "Afterward you will take me into glory" (v. 24). It is the *certain reality of heaven.* The arrival of the time when God will wipe away every tear from our eyes. When there will be no more death or mourning, crying, or pain. When the old order passes away and we hear Him say, "I am making everything new!" (Revelation 21:4-5).

Don Wyrtzen has captured the strength of the coming prosperity of heaven in his song *Finally Home.*

When engulfed by the terror of
tempestuous sea,
Unknown waves before you roll;

At the end of doubt and peril is
    eternity,
Though fear and conflict seize
    your soul:
When surrounded by the blackness of
    the darkest night,
O how lonely death can be;
At the end of this long tunnel is a
    shining light,
For death is swallowed up in victory!
But just think of stepping on shore
    and finding it heaven!
Of touching a hand and finding it God's!
Of breathing new air and finding it
    celestial!
Of waking up in glory and finding it home!

The psalmist concludes his discourse on true prosperity by rejoicing in his God.

Whom have I in heaven but you?
    And earth has nothing I desire besides you.
My flesh and my heart may fail,
    but God is the strength of my heart
    and my portion forever.

Those who are far from you will perish;
    you will destroy all who are unfaithful to you.
But as for me, it is good to be near God.
    I have made the Sovereign Lord my refuge;
    I will tell of all your deeds.
                (Psalm 73:25-28)

True prosperity is found in God's in-depth, long-range goodness to His people. The wicked do not prosper. Not really.

13

Keep On Keeping On
Perseverance

The bumper sticker read, "When the going gets tough the tough go shopping!"

It is tough to hang in there when things are tough. Shopping would be a nice alternative. Nevertheless, one of the frustrating things about pain is that it's impossible to walk away from it. You must stay in the ring and seek to survive, seek to conquer, seek to win. That requires stick-to-itiveness. And sticking to it requires perseverance.

I left seminary several years ago with an unflinching commitment to the doctrine of the perseverance of the saints. I soon discovered that on a practical level, the saints don't persevere all that well. As a young pastor, I noted that God's flock was often more committed to comfort than to character, to convenience more than to commitment, to cash more than to Christ. It was a unique brand of disposable discipleship. A Christianity that was good in pleasure, but not good in pain—so I hammered away in the pulpit, trying to call God's people to perseverance.

In time, I encountered a few difficulties. Now, to my surprise, I didn't persevere all that well myself. I found that when the going got tough, I was prone to wander—spiritually, mentally, and emotionally.

Runners have friends along the way who throw them towels or hand them cups of something to drink.

We need a fresh call for the stick-to-itiveness of the saints. Saints who refuse to curse God in pain. Who refuse bitterness. Who refuse to "go it alone." Who refuse to buy the recommendations and remedies of the world. Who claim righteousness as their ultimate cause in every situation. Who say with Job, "The Lord gave and the Lord has taken away; may the name of the Lord be praised" (Job 1:21). Who affirm Job's faith personally. The faith that claims, "Though he slay me, yet will I hope in him" (Job 13:15). Who kneel with Christ in their Garden of Gethsemane and pray as He prayed that the cup be removed, and yet with a unique yieldedness surrender their will to the will of the Father. Who find that God's grace is sufficient. Who go for the grace, look for the growth, and live for the glory.

PERSEVERANCE IS THE KEY

Keeping on in a crisis requires that we have the steady and solid foundation of perseverance. The author of Hebrews exhorts his readers who were under severe pressure, "Therefore, since we are surrounded by such a great cloud of witnesses, let us throw off everything that hinders and the sin that so easily entangles, and let us run with perseverance the race marked out for us" (Hebrews 12:1). The race marked out for them was an obstacle course. It required that they face the obstacles of rejection, loss of friends, economic difficulty, and daily persecution. Perseverance would be their indispensable companion in trouble.

I have friends who are runners. They have kindled my interest in marathons, those massive, grueling twenty-six-mile runs. As I have watched some of the races, I have noted that the runners have friends along the way who throw them towels or hand them cups of something to drink. I sense that these companions are essential to the runners' success. It's like that with perseverance. You can't run the course of trouble without it.

As we have seen, the word *perseverance* is literally made up of two words. One meaning "to remain." The other word meaning "under." This is the essence of perseverance. It is the ability to stay under the pressure of our difficulty with a good spirit. We usually want to squirt out from under the pressure. To be done. To hurry the sunshine.

God intends that we, in time, will blossom under pressure. Perseverance gives God the time to do His work of blossoming through us. That's why James exhorts us to submit to the trial and let perseverance "finish its work" (James 1:4). Refusing to persevere aborts the work of God that is being conceived in us.

Pressure comes in many different forms. For you, it may be the pressure of continued physical pain. Emotional distress. The breaking up of a valued relationship. Rejection by peers. A wayward child. A struggle with temptation. A haunting from your past. The pull of priorities. Overwhelming responsibilities. Economic stress. Demolished dreams. It may be, as Paul writes, that you are pressed on every side (2 Corinthians 4:8).

There is an ancient torture in which the sufferer is literally "drawn and quartered." A horse is tied to each ankle and each wrist of the victim. Then the horses are marched slowly away from one another, each in a different direction. There are times in our lives when pressures and problems seem to be ripping us apart, times when we feel "drawn and quartered."

But in it all, there is one constant reality that keeps our heads above the flood—and that is perseverance. The ability to stay under the pressure until the pain has resulted in God's gain. How is perseverance developed? What is at the core?

THE STRENGTH OF PERSEVERANCE

Hebrews 11 provides a roster of saints who persevered under phenomenal pressure. It is a listing of some of those who metaphorically compose the great "cloud of witnesses" that now surround us. Near the conclusion to that chapter, the writer of the book summarizes some of their trials:

> Women received back their dead, raised to life again. Others were tortured and refused to be released, so that they might gain a better resurrection. Some faced jeers and flogging, while still others were chained and put in prison. They were stoned; they were sawed in two; they were put to death by the sword. They went about in sheepskins and goatskins, destitute, persecuted and mistreated—the world was not worthy of them. They wandered in deserts and mountains, and in caves and holes in the ground. (Hebrews 11:35-38)

Somehow their experiences helps put my problems into perspective. Not that mine hurt any less, but in their lives I get a glimpse of true perseverance.

Note the commentary on their lives: "These were all commended for their faith" (v. 39). They persevered. They got a good report. A "well done, thou good and faithful servant" (Matthew 25:21, KJV). What was at the center of their commendation? Their *faith*. It was the very essence, the strength of their perseverance.

Have faith, brother! is the exhortation of Hebrews 11. Faith always has an object, something it attaches itself to. Our faith is only as good as the source to which it clings. You can nail, glue, bolt, reinforce, and permanently fasten a support beam to a wall. But if the wall falls down, the support beam is no good.

We have a "know so" faith.

God is our solid, unshakable, sure support in trouble. No weight can pull Him down. As we have learned, faith means grabbing hold of His character and believing that He is good, all-powerful, caring, forgiving, tender, and just. True faith refuses to let go of those realities. Faith means taking God's promises, claiming them, and clinging to them. It is grasping His Word and applying it to our pain. Although faith does not always give us answers, it does always keep us steady and secure. It focuses our hearts and minds on the light at the end of the tunnel, the light of God's glory revealed in us.

As I review this tremendous cast of suffering saints, I ask myself, *In what did they place their faith?* I noticed a common thread. They all suffered as a part of God's *plan*. They believed He had a *purpose* for their lives. He had promised them a plan, and though it didn't materialize until after they went to be with Him (Hebrews 11:39), they affirmed it in their lives and refused to bail out.

MOTIVATION TO PERSEVERE

The Old Testament saints suffered without seeing the promise of the Messiah fulfilled. They went through their deep waters with only a "hope so" faith. They were willing to do their part for what was yet to come.

But "God had planned something better for us so that only together with us would they be made perfect" (Hebrews 11:40).

We have a "know so" faith. Christ has come. All that the Old Testament saints suffered to conceive has been born through our Savior. He has conquered sin, death, hell, suffering, and sorrow. We are on the victory side. We do our part for Him in pain or pleasure, blessing and buffeting, with the *confidence* of His victory.

Not only do we have a better way, but we also play a part in completing what the Old Testament saints have begun. As the plan of God stretches from age to age, some saints in years gone by invested their lives to make possible that which is to come. Those who follow complete that which others have begun. In the scope of biblical history we are much like the last runner in a relay race. Throughout the Old Testament, many people suffered to preserve and produce the Messiah seed. Christ suffered to conquer sin and death and to provide the message of eternal life. The apostles and the first-century church suffered greatly to plant God's church.

> *And so I look. He is there. . . . It is Jesus, the author and finisher of my faith. The One who, for the joy set before Him, endured the cross.*

Now it's our turn. We take our places. We are completers. We perfect what they have begun. In a real sense, when we refuse to persevere, when we refuse to do our part in God's plan and purpose, we abort what they suffered to conceive.

I am motivated when I think that I am not in this alone. Like a runner in the last lap of a relay race, I am motivated to successfully complete what those who went before worked so hard to begin. I am a part of God's grand big picture. I will do my part. I too will be faithful in good times and bad. I want God to count on me!

MY TURN

Hebrews 12:1 ushers me into a great Roman arena. The Holy Spirit hands me the baton, and now I must run the race marked for me. I notice that the track is an obstacle course, full of the pitfalls of the world system. I see more buffetings than blessings on the track ahead of me, and I say, "I can't do it! Not me, Lord."

As I begin to hand the baton back, I see the great crowd that fills the arena. They all have run before and persevered. They all have finished triumphantly by faith. They did their part in their day.

I see Abel, killed for righteousness. Joseph and David are there. Job. Moses, the one who forsook fame, fortune, and pleasure for God. Jeremiah, who wept. Prophets who were rejected and stoned. Peter, crucified upside down in Rome. Stephen. The five missionaries murdered by the Auca Indians. They are all calling to me, "Joe, keep on keeping on! Do your part. Complete what we through suffering have begun. Run, Joe, run!"

As I pull the baton back and clutch it tightly, I remember that in every Roman arena there was an emperor's box. An athlete coming onto the field would always look to see if the emperor was watching. And so I look. He is there. I fix my eyes on Him. It is Jesus, the author and finisher of my faith. The One who, for the joy set before Him, endured the cross (Hebrews 12:2).

As I step onto the track, my mind focuses on all those who have gone before me. I think of David Livingstone, the pioneer missionary to Africa, who walked over twenty-nine thousand miles. His wife died early in their ministry, and he faced stiff opposition from his Scottish brethren. He ministered half-blind. His kind of perseverance spurs me on. As I run, I remember the words in his diary:

> Send me anywhere, only go with me. Lay any burden on me, only sustain me. Sever me from any tie but the tie that binds one to Your service and to Your heart.

And I remember the penetrating words of Isaac Watts:

> Am I a soldier of the cross,
>   A foll'wer of the Lamb,
> And shall I fear to own His cause,
>   Or blush to speak His name?
>
> Must I be carried to the skies
>   On flowery beds of ease,
> While others fought to win the prize,
>   And sailed thro' bloody seas?
>
> Are there no foes for me to face?
>   Must I not stem the flood?
> Is this vile world a friend to grace,
>   To help me on to God?
>
> Sure I must fight, if I would reign;
>   Increase my courage, Lord.
> I'll bear the toil, endure the pain,
>   Supported by Thy Word.

Dr. Joseph Stowell can be heard each week on the "Moody Presents" radio broadcast, aired on over two hundred stations worldwide. Call your local Christian radio station for date and time of airing. Cassettes of Dr. Stowell's pulpit ministry are available from the MBN Cassette Ministry and can be ordered by calling (312) 329-8010, Monday through Friday between 7:30 A.M. and 9:30 P.M. Central time.